THE PEOPLE OF THE SCOTTISH BURGHS

A Genealogical Source Book

The People of Dumfries
1600-1799

D1542164

By David Dobson

CLEARFIELD

Printed for Clearfield Company by
Genealogical Publishing Company
Baltimore, Maryland
2015

ISBN 978-0-8063-5778-2

INTRODUCTION

Dumfries is and was the most important burgh in south west Scotland and dominates the trade of the area known as Dumfries and Galloway. Dumfries was established as a Royal Burgh by King William I of Scotland in 1186. The site of the burgh was the upper tidal limit and the location of the lowest bridging point on the River Nith. Strategically it controlled the road west to the coast and ports linking to Ireland, and it was from where much of the seaborne trade of the region was conducted. Since the medieval period Dumfries, lying near the confluence of the River Nith and the Solway Firth, had been involved in both coastal and overseas trade, and from the late seventeenth century trade with the Baltic and with the Americas increased substantially. This trade led to emigration initially to Ireland but especially to North America and the West Indies. As a burgh Dumfries was semi-autonomous with a council elected by the burgesses, who were an urban elite representing about ten per cent of the adult males there and mainly the merchants and craftsmen. This genealogical source books identifies many of the inhabitants of the burgh of Dumfries of the seventeenth and eighteenth centuries and is overwhelmingly based on primary sources. It is designed to provide information which would enhance the basic data of baptisms, marriages, and sometimes deaths found in the Old Parish Registers of the Church of Scotland. A range of documentary sources have been located such as testaments, deeds, sasines [property], marriage contracts, bonds, court records, customs references, letter-books, and others, all of which provide a useful insight into the lives of the people of the period. Among the inhabitants listed here is Robert Burns, the national poet, who lies buried in the kirkyard of St Michael's. The major families in Dumfries and its neighborhood were the Maxwells, the Johnstons, the Griersons, the Carruthers, the Charteris, the Kirkpatricks, the Irvines, the Jardines, and the Carlyles, names which are well represented in this book.

David Dobson

Dundee, Scotland, 2015.

REFERENCES

AJ	=	Aberdeen Journal
ANY	=	St Andrew's Society of New York
BM	=	Blackwood's Magazine
BRO	=	Bristol Records Office
CLC	=	Calendar of the Laing Charters 854-1837
Comm.	=	Commissariat
DAC	=	Dumfries Archive Centre
DBR	=	Dumfries Burgh Records
EA	=	Edinburgh Advertiser
EMA	=	Emigrant Ministers to America
EUL	=	Edinburgh University Library
F	=	Fasti Ecclesiae Scoticanae
FPA	=	Fulham Papers, American
LC	=	Calendar of the Laing Charters
LPR	=	List of Prisoners of the Rebellion
MdGaz		Maryland Gazette
MI	=	Monumental Inscription
MSA	=	Maryland State Archives
NEHGS		New England Historical Genealogical Society
NLS	=	National Library of Scotland, Edinburgh
NRS	=	National Records of Scotland, Edinburgh
NYGaz		New York Gazette

OSC	=	Old Scottish Clockmakers, 1453-1850
Pa	=	Port of Ayr, 1727-1780
RGS	=	Register of the Great Seal of Scotland
RPCS	=	Register of the Privy Council of Scotland
SCGaz		South Carolina Gazette
SCHR		Scottish Church History Review
SM	=	Scots Magazine
TDG	=	Transactions of the Dumfries and Galloway Nat. Hist. Soc.
TNA	=	The National Archives, London
VaGaz	=	Virginia Gazette
VMHB		Virginia Magazine of History and Biography

GLOSSARY

Bailie	=	a magistrate
Baxter	=	a baker
Chapman	=	a pedlar
Cordiner	=	a leather worker
Covenanter	=	a militant Presbyterian
Flax-dresser	=	a textile worker
Flesher	=	a butcher
Hammerman	=	a metal worker
Hucker	=	a hawker
Limner	=	a painter
Litster	=	a dyer
Maltster	=	a brewer
Maltman	=	a brewer
Ormond Pursuivant	=	a herald
Provost	=	a mayor
Relict	=	a widow
Sasine	=	a property transaction
Squareman	=	a mason
Tide-waiter	=	a Customs officer
Tolbooth	=	a jail
Webster	=	a weaver
Writer	=	a lawyer

ADAMSON, JOHN, in Rigside, parish of Dumfries, testament, 1638, Comm. Dumfries. [NRS]

ADAMSON, JOHN, son of the late John Adamson, a merchant burgess of Dumfries, testament, 1657, Comm. Dumfries. [NRS]

ADAMSON, MARGARET, spouse of Robert Wright a carrier burgess of Dumfries, testament, 1681, Comm. Dumfries. [NRS]

ADAMSON, ROBERT, was admitted as a burgess of Dumfries in 1726. [DBR]

ADAMSON, THOMAS, a merchant, was admitted as a burgess of Dumfries in 1770. [DBR]

AFFLECK, ALEXANDER, a mason, was admitted as a burgess of Dumfries in 1737, [DBR]; a mason and late Deacon Convenor of the Trades of Dumfries, testament, 14 March 1777. [NRS.CC5/6]

AFFLECK, ELIZABETH, daughter of Samuel Affleck a mason in Dumfries, and his wife Agnes Lithgow, testament, 1783, Comm. Dumfries. [NRS]

AFFLECK, JAMES, was admitted as a burgess of Dumfries in 1727. [DBR]

AFFLECK, JAMES, a minister, sometime in Middelburg, Zealand, thereafter in Aldergate, London, and lately in Dumfries, testament, 25 April 1800. [NRS.CC5/6]

AFFLECK, SAMUEL, born 1739, a mason, was admitted as a burgess of Dumfries in 1773. [DBR]; died 28 February 1804, spouse of Agnes Lithgow. [St Michael's MI]

AFFLECK, WILLIAM, late Deacon of the Squaremen in Dumfries, testament, 11 April 1746. [NRS.CC5/6]

A'HANNAY, WILLIAM, a burgess of Dumfries, a bond, 1616. [NRS.GD6.1809]

AITKEN ADAM, in Dumfries, testament, 1799, Comm. Dumfries. [NRS]

AITKEN, ANDREW, burgess of Dumfries, testament, 18 April 1643, Comm. Dumfries.. [NRS.CC5/6]

AITKEN, HUGH, carter in Bridgend of Dumfries, testament, 23 July 1782. [NRS.CC5/6]

AITKEN, JAMES, and his son James, merchants at the Bridgend of Dumfries, sasines, 27 February 1703 and 24 January 1711. [NRS.RS23.6/398, 8/10]

AITKEN, JAMES, an innkeeper at the Bridgend of Dumfries, 1775. [NRS.RS23.XXI.56/273]

AITKEN, JOHN, merchant burgess of Dumfries, testament, 12 July 1679. [NRS.CC5/6]

AITKEN, JOHN, a writer, was admitted as a burgess of Dumfries in 1754. [DBR]; sheriff-substitute of Dumfries and factor or chamberlain for the burgh of Dumfries, testaments, 7 October and 30 November 1796. [NRS.CC5/6]

AITKEN, ROGER, a merchant, was admitted as a burgess of Dumfries in 1738. [DBR]; a merchant in Dumfries, 1786. [NRS.CE51.Letterbook]

ALEXANDER, ELIZABETH, spouse to Thomas Veitch a barber and periwig maker in Dumfries, testament, 24 June 1730. [NRS.CC5/6]

ALEXANDER, JOHN, master of the Adventure of Dumfries, bound for Danzig and France, 1680s. [NAS.E72.6.7/8/9/10]

ALEXANDER, ROBERT, from Dumfries, a member of the Scots Charitable Society of Boston in 1758. [NEHGS/SCSpp]

ALISON, ROBERT, weaver in Dumfries, testament, 13 March 1745. [NRS.5/6]

ALLAN, BENJAMIN, a merchant, was admitted as a burgess of Dumfries in 1750. [DBR]

ALLAN, FRANCIS, a mason, was admitted as a burgess of Dumfries in 1759. [DBR]

ALLAN, JANET, resident in Dumfries, widow of William Ferguson a merchant in Dumfries, testament, 8 July 1799. [NRS.CC5/6]

ALLAN, JOHN, a weaver, was admitted as a burgess of Dumfries in 1766. [DBR]

ALLAN, PATRICK, with his wife Janet Vetch, and their son James Allan arrived in Dumfries from Ireland by 1696. [NRS.CH2.537.1/161-165]

ALLAN, WILLIAM, a wigmaker and barber in Dumfries, his wife Mary Smith, and son James, a sasine, 19 June 1728. [NRS.RS23.10.386]

ANDERSON, DAVID, a shoemaker, was admitted as a burgess of Dumfries in 1743. [DBR]

ANDERSON, HOMER, Deacon of the Fleshers of Dumfries, 1661. [DAC]

ANDERSON, HOMER, was admitted as a burgess of Dumfries in 1727. [DBR]

ANDERSON, HOMER, a brewer, was admitted as a burgess of Dumfries in 1738. [DBR]

ANDERSON, JAMES, was admitted as a burgess of Dumfries in 1724. [DBR]

ANDERSON, JAMES, a shoemaker, was admitted as a burgess of Dumfries in 1750. [DBR]

ANDERSON, JAMES, a shopkeeper, was admitted as a burgess of Dumfries in 1762. [DBR]

ANDERSON, JAMES, a wright, was admitted as a burgess of Dumfries in 1772. [DBR]

ANDERSON, JAMES, sr., a merchant in Dumfries, testament, 1785, Comm. Dumfries. [NRS]

ANDERSON, JAMES, jr., a merchant in Dumfries, testament, 1786, Comm. Dumfries. [NRS]

ANDERSON, JAMES, a stocking-maker, was admitted as a burgess of Dumfries in 1792. [DBR]

ANDERSON, JANET, spouse to Thomas Kirkpatrick, in the parish of Dumfries, testament, 1641, Comm. Dumfries. [NRS]

ANDERSON, JANET, a widow who arrived in Dumfries from Ireland in 1691. [NRS.CH2.537.15.1/73-94]

ANDERSON, JOHN, emigrated from Dumfries to Virginia aboard the Nanie and Jenny, master William Maxwell, 23 May 1749. [NRS.CS96.2161.9]

ANDERSON, MICHAEL, a tailor burgess of Dumfries, 1601. [RPCS.VI.263]

ANDERSON, NICHOLAS, a merchant, was admitted as a burgess of Dumfries in 1762. [DBR]

ANDERSON, ROBERT, a merchant in Dumfries, 1621. [NRS.E71.10.5]

ANDERSON, ROBERT, a merchant in Dumfries, a sasine, 11 October 1709.
[NRS.RS23.7.440]

ANDERSON, ROBERT, was admitted as a burgess of Dumfries in 1728.
[DBR]

ANDERSON, ROBERT, jr., was admitted as a burgess of Dumfries in 1738.
[DBR]

ANDERSON, ROBERT, a dyer, was admitted as a burgess of Dumfries in 1738.
[DBR]

ANDERSON, RODGER, a burgess of Dumfries, testament, 1673, Comm.
Dumfries. [NRS]

ANDERSON, WILLIAM, born in Dumfries, a planter in St Joseph's parish,
Georgia, probate 7 February 1772, Georgia.

APPLEBY, JAMES, a merchant, was admitted as a burgess of Dumfries in
1765. [DBR]; testament, 1798, Comm. Dumfries. [NRS]

ARCHIBALD, GEORGE, MD in Dumfries, a deed, 1702, his wife Marion,
daughter Margaret, sasines, 1703-1716. [NRS.RD4.90.140/721; RS23.6/407;
7/436, 438; 8/58, 156; 9/48]

ARMSTRONG, CHRISTOPHER, a shop-keeper, was admitted as a burgess of
Dumfries in 1799. [DBR]

ARMSTRONG, JOHN, a wright, was admitted as a burgess of Dumfries in
1750. [DBR]

ARMSTRONG, JOHN, an innkeeper, was admitted as a burgess of Dumfries in
1770. [DBR]

ARMSTRONG, J., a writer, was admitted as a burgess of Dumfries in 1792.
[DBR]

ARMSTRONG, ROBERT, a tailor, was admitted as a burgess of Dumfries in
1751. [DBR]

ARCHIBALD, MARGARET, daughter of Dr George Archibald in Dumfries,
and widow of Gabriel Allason of Dunjap, a sasine, 19 November 1711.
[NRS.RS23.8/58]

ARMSTRONG, WILLIAM, a merchant in Dumfries, 1621. [NRS.E71.10.5]

ARMSTRONG, WILLIAM, a prisoner in Dumfries jail, accused of cattle theft, 1634. [RPCS.V.302]

ARMSTRONG, WILLIAM, was admitted as a burgess of Dumfries in 1726. [DBR]

ARTHUR, HARBERT, a cooper burgess of Dumfries, testament, 1625, Comm. Dumfries. [NRS]

ASHTON, ELIZABETH, in Dumfries, will, 1778. [NRS.GD2.73]

AULD, WALTER, was admitted as a burgess of Dumfries in 1784. [DBR]; a saddler in Dumfries, 1793. [NRS.CS233.SEQN.A1.3]

BAILLIE, JAMES, late Customs clerk in Dumfries, 1691. [RPCS.XIII,459]

BAILLIE, ROBERT, was admitted as a burgess of Dumfries in 1648. [DBR] a merchant baillie of Dumfries, testament, 1685, Comm. Dumfries. [NRS]

BAILLIE, ROBERT, an Excise officer in Dumfries, testament, 1764, Comm. Dumfries. [NRS]

BAILIFF, JOSEPH, a shopkeeper, was admitted as a burgess of Dumfries in 1787. [DBR]

BARCLAY, ALEXANDER, was admitted as a burgess of Dumfries in 1699 [DBR]; a merchant bailie of Dumfries, formerly a skipper there, sasines, 1710-1722. [NRS.RS23.7/469; 9/283; 10/5]; bailie of Dumfries, 1707. [EUL.LC3036]

BARNS, THOMAS, a shoemaker, was admitted as a burgess of Dumfries in 1745. [DBR]

BARRY, CHARLES, was admitted as a burgess of Dumfries in 1770. [DBR]

BARRY, THOMAS, an earthen-ware merchant, was admitted as a burgess of Dumfries in 1744. [DBR]; an earthenware merchant in Dumfries, 1753. [NRS.CS231.B1.33]

BARTON, HUGH, Deacon of the Wrights in Dumfries, testament [missing], 1699, 1700, Comm. Dumfries. [NRS]

BARTON, JEAN, spouse of John Lawson a merchant burgess of Dumfries, testament, 1675, Comm. Dumfries. [NRS]

BATTIE, JOHN, a merchant in Dumfries, 1621. [NRS.E71.10.5]

BAXTER, ALEXANDER, son of Thomas Baxter a wright in Dumfries, testament, 1769, Comm. Dumfries. [NRS]

BAXTER, DAVID, a merchant in Dumfries, 1622. [NRS.E71.10.5]

BAXTER, GILBERT, a wright in Dumfries, testament, 1775, Comm. Dumfries. [NRS]

BAXTER, WILLIAM, a wright, was admitted as a burgess of Dumfries in 1740. [DBR]

BEAN, DAVID, a merchant in Dumfries, a petition, 1772. [NRS.CS238.B.3.8]; testament, 1792, Comm. Dumfries. [NRS]

BEATTIE, FRANCIS, a dyer, was admitted as a burgess of Dumfries in 1799. [DBR]

BEATTIE, ROBERT, an accountant in Dumfries, testament, 1795, Comm. Dumfries. [NRS]

BEATTIE, THOMAS, a merchant burgess of Dumfries, testament, 1638, Comm. Dumfries. [NRS]

BEATTIE, WILLIAM, apprentice to Irving Logan in Dumfries, absconded to Virginia, 1737. [NRS.CH2.537.2.84]

BEATTIE, WILLIAM, a merchant from Dumfries, settled in Virginia by 1749, a merchant in Petersburg, Va., by 1770. [NRS.CS1.81; VaGaz.1006/1046/1280]

BECK, GEORGE, was admitted as a burgess of Dumfries in 1689. [DBR]; a merchant in Dumfries, a deed, 1714. [NRS.RD4.114.1234]

BECK, JOHN, a cordiner at the Bridgend of Dumfries, testament, 1683, Comm. Dumfries. [NRS]

BECK, MARGARET, spouse of Thomas Sharp a merchant burgess of Dumfries, testament, 1627, Comm. Dumfries. [NRS]

BECK, MARION, spouse to Thomas Wright a merchant burgess of Dumfries, testament, 1638, Comm. Dumfries. [NRS]

BECK, ROBERT, residing in Dumfries, suspected of Catholicism, 1601. [RPCS.VI.312]

BECK, WILLIAM, son of James Beck, [1770-1822] a carter in Dumfries, and his wife Sophia Bell, died in Quebec aged 29. [Dumfries MI]

BEE, JAMES, master of the Jenny of Dumfries, 1786. [NRS.CE51.Letterbook]

BELL, ANDREW, a wheelwright, was admitted as a burgess of Dumfries in 1768. [DBR]

BELL, BENJAMIN, master of the Peggy of Dumfries, trading with Virginia, 1752. [NRS.E504.9.2]

BELL, BENJAMIN, a writer, was admitted as a burgess of Dumfries in 1797. [DBR]

BELL, DAVID, a wheelwright, sometime in Dumfries, later in Amisfieldtown, testament, 1785, Comm. Dumfries. [NRS]

BELL, FRANCIS, a shoemaker, was admitted as a burgess of Dumfries in 1757. [DBR]

BELL, GEORGE, a merchant in Dumfries, a sasine, 7 June 1727. [NRS.RS23.10.292]; a merchant in Dumfries, trading with Dublin in 1746. [NRS.E504.9.1]

BELL, GEORGE, jr., a merchant, was admitted as a burgess of Dumfries in 1746. [DBR]

BELL, GEORGE, a writer, was admitted as a burgess of Dumfries in 1722. [DBR]; Provost of Dumfries, 1745. [NRS.GD18.3246/3250]

BELL, GEORGE, a skinner, was admitted as a burgess of Dumfries in 1761. [DBR]

BELL, JAMES, was admitted as a burgess of Dumfries in 1716. [DBR]; a merchant in Dumfries, a sasine, 7 June 1727. [NRS.RS23.10.292]

BELL, JANET, spouse of John Brown a tailor in Dumfries, testament, 1686, Comm. Dumfries. [NRS]

BELL, NICOL, a tailor in Dumfries, testament, 1745, Comm. Dumfries. [NRS]

BELL, ROBERT, master of the Robert of Dumfries, 1690.
[NRS.E72.6.18/20/21]

BELL, ROBERT, a merchant in Dumfries, testament [missing], 1714, Comm.
Dumfries. [NRS]

BELL, ROBERT, a joiner, was admitted as a burgess of Dumfries in 1771.
[DBR]

BELL, THOMAS, a prisoner in Dumfries jail, accused of cattle theft, 1634.
[RPCS.V.302]

BELL, THOMAS, master of the Queensberry of Dumfries bound for Virginia,
February 1754. [NRS.E504.22.5]_

BELL, WILLIAM, a merchant, was admitted as a burgess of Dumfries in 1740.
[DBR]; testament, 1768, Comm. Dumfries. [NRS]

BELL, WILLIAM, in Dumfries, letters, 1755-1756. [NRS.RH15.66.3]

BELL, WILLIAM, an innkeeper in Dumfries, testaments, 1790, 1791, 1793,
Comm. Dumfries. [NRS]

BELLIS, DAVID, a merchant in Dumfries, trading with Flanders, 1622.
[NAS.E71.10.5]

BENNET, JOHN, a weaver in Dumfries, his wife Elizabeth Lawson, and son
John, sasines, 1707-1730. [NRS.RS23.7/255, 256; 11/13]

BENNOCH, SAMUEL, a tailor, was admitted as a burgess of Dumfries in
1740. [DBR]

BERRY, WILLIAM, a glover, was admitted as a burgess of Dumfries in 1762.
[DBR]

BIGGAR, JAMES, born 1779 in Dumfries, son of John Biggar in
Fourmerkland, a merchant who died 25 June 1804 in Greenwich,
Kingston. [Kingston MI, Jamaica]

BIGGAR, JOHN, a tailor, was admitted as a burgess of Dumfries in 1738.
[DBR]

BIGGAR, ROBERT, a tanner, was admitted as a burgess of Dumfries in 1783.
[DBR]

BISHOP, DAVID, was admitted as a burgess of Dumfries in 1660. [DBR]; late Provost of Dumfries, testament, 1680, Comm. Dumfries. [NRS] died 7 October 1679, husband of Janet Cunningham. [St Michael's MI, Dumfries]

BISHOP, DAVID, provost of Dumfries, sasines, 1721. [NRS.RS23.9/311-314]

BISHOP. ISOBEL, daughter of David Bishop the Provost of Dumfries, and relict of John McCulloch, sasines, 1711/1721. [NRS.RS23.8/12; 9/312]

BISHOP, JAMES, was admitted as a burgess of Dumfries in 1678. [DBR]; a merchant in Dumfries, sasines, 1703/1711/1721. [NRS.RS23.6/398; 8/10-12; 9/313]

BISHOP, JOHN, a merchant in Dumfries, a sasine, 25 December 1717. [NRS.RS23.9/128]

BLACK, JOHN, was admitted as a burgess of Dumfries in 1701. [DBR];a merchant in Dumfries, 1708, 1721, 1727. [NRS.AC9.313; AC9.764; AC8.353]

BLACK, MARGARET, spouse of William Logan, in Dumfries, a sasine, 1729. [NRS.GD1.202.62]

BLACK, WILLIAM, born 1679 in Dumfries, a minister in Accomack County, Virginia, 1708. [SCHR.14.149][EMA14] [FPA173]

BLACKLAND, WILLIAM, a tailor in Dumfries, subscribed to the Test, 1683. [RPCS.VIII.640]

BLACKLOCK, ANNE, a mantua maker in Dumfries, testament, 1758, Comm. Dumfries. [NRS]

BLACKLOCK, JOHN, a merchant in Dumfries, 1621. [NAS.E71.10.5]

BLACKLOCK, JOHN, a merchant, was admitted as a burgess of Dumfries in 1755. [DBR]

BLACKLOCK, MARION, wife of Gilbert Crockett a merchant in Dumfries, testament, 1687, Comm. Dumfries. [NRS]

BLACKLOCK, THOMAS, a shoemaker, was admitted as a burgess of Dumfries in 1764. [DBR]

BLACKSTOCK, ANDREW, an ostler, was admitted as a burgess of Dumfries in 1757. [DBR]

BLACKSTOCK, BESSIE, relict of Herbert Caird a merchant in Dumfries, testament, 1674, Comm. Dumfries. [NRS]

BLACKSTOCK, JOHN, a merchant burgess of Dumfries, testament, 1641, Comm. Dumfries. [NRS]

BLACKSTOCK, JOHN, a shoemaker in Dumfries, 1727. [NRS.AC9.1015]

BLACKSTOCK, JOHN, a shoemaker, late deacon convenor of the Trades of Dumfries, testaments, 1788, 1798, Comm. Dumfries. [NRS]

BLACKSTOCK, MARION, relict of Thomas Bridge a merchant in Dumfries, a sasine, 11 August 1724. [NRS; 9/274; 10/81/277/287]S.RS23.10/132]; testament, 1741, Comm. Dumfries. [NRS]

BLACKSTOCK, ROBERT, a shoemaker, was admitted as a burgess of Dumfries in 1722. [DBR]; testament, 1738, Comm. Dumfries. [NRS]

BLAIR, ALEXANDER, sailor aboard the Mally of Dumfries which was captured by an American privateer when bound for Nova Scotia in 1776 but was later liberated by the Royal Navy in 1777. [NRS.AC7.60]

BLAIR, DAVID, master of the Lilly of Dumfries, trading with Virginia in 1750, 1752. [NRS.E504.9.2][VaGaz.94]

BLAIR, DAVID, Customs Controller in Dumfries, versus ...... McCourtrie in Jamaica, 29 July 1778. [NRS.CS16.1.174]

BLAIR, DAVID, of Beltenmont, late Provost of Dumfries, testaments, 1794, 1795, Comm. Dumfries. [NRS]

BLAIR, JOHN, a joiner, was admitted as a burgess of Dumfries in 1769. [DBR]

BLAIR, WILLIAM, a tobacconist at the Bridgend of Dumfries,1786. [NRS.CE51.Letterbook]

BLAKE, ADAM, a gardener, was admitted as a burgess of Dumfries in 1767. [DBR]

BLAKE, ANDREW, an innkeeper in Dumfries, testament, 1757, Comm. Dumfries. [NRS]

BLAND, ROBERT, a merchant, was admitted as a burgess of Dumfries in 1798. [DBR]

BLOUNT, GEORGE, son of David Blount an innkeeper in Dumfries, an apprentice indenture, 1731. [NRS.GD1.1261.3]

BLUNT, GEORGE, a merchant, was admitted as a burgess of Dumfries in 1750. [DBR]

BLOUNT, ROBERT, son of James Blount, a farmer in Rosedale, [1756-1816], and his wife Marie Kissock, died July 1823 in Jamaica. [Dumfries MI]

BLOUNT, SAMUEL, born 1794, son of Lieutenant David Blount, died in September 1828 in Jamaica. [Dumfries MI]

BODDEN, WILLIAM, a wright, was admitted as a burgess of Dumfries in 1769. [DBR]

BOGLE, JAMES, a gardener, was admitted as a burgess of Dumfries in 1767.. [DBR]

BORTHWICK, JOHN, a tailor, was admitted as a burgess of Dumfries in 1750. [DBR]

BOYD, ELIZABETH, in Dumfries, relict of William Birkmyre in New Abbey, testament, 1744, Comm.Dumfries. NRS]

BOYD, GEORGE, a maltster, was admitted as a burgess of Dumfries in 1743. [DBR]; testament, 1753, Comm. Dumfries. [NRS]

BOYD, JAMES, at the Bridgend of Dumfries, testament, 1658, Comm. Dumfries. [NRS]

BOYD, JOHN, a stocking-maker, was admitted as a burgess of Dumfries in 1771. [DBR]

BOYD, ROBERT, arrived in Dumfries from Ireland in 1690.
[NRS.CH2.537.15.1/34]

BOYD, ROBERT, a writer in Dumfries, sasines, 1719-1727.
[NRS.RS23.9/181]; 1707, [eul.lc.3606]

BOYD, WILLIAM, a bookseller, was admitted as a burgess of Dumfries in
1769. [DBR]

BRAIDEN, ROBERT, born 1737, a labourer from Dumfries, with
his wife Jean Kirkpatrick, born Dumfries. 1749, and sons James,
born 1768, twins William and David born 1771, and Edward, born
1774, emigrated to Prince Edward Island aboard the Lovely Nelly
in May 1775. [TNA.T47.12]

BRAITHWAITE, JEAN, relict of William Scott of Beltenmont, a
vintner in Dumfries, testament, 1750, Comm. Dumfries. [NRS]

BRAND, JAMES, a merchant, was admitted as a burgess of Dumfries in 1740.
[DBR]

BRAND, JAMES, [1781-1840], a merchant in Dumfries, husband
of Jean McQueen, parents of James Brand, a merchant in New
York. [Dumfries MI]

BRAND, WILLIAM, a merchant, was admitted as a burgess of Dumfries in
1716. [DBR]

BRAND, WILLIAM, an innkeeper, was admitted as a burgess of Dumfries in
1768. [DBR]

BRATTON, ROBERT, a workman, was admitted as a burgess of Dumfries in
1743. [DBR]

BRAYEN, JAMES, a shopkeeper, was admitted as a burgess of Dumfries in
1769. [DBR]

BRECK, JAMES, a tobacconist, was admitted as a burgess of Dumfries in
1760. [DBR]

BROADFOOT, WILLIAM, a shoemaker, was admitted as a burgess of
Dumfries in 1744. [DBR]

BROATCH, JOHN, was admitted as a burgess of Dumfries in 1666. [DBR]; former Dean of Dumfries, testament, 1691, Comm. Dumfries. [NRS]

BROATCH, MARGARET, relict of Robert Newall a weaver in Dumfries, testament, 1725. Comm. Dumfries. [NRS]

BROOM, THOMAS, a baxter, was admitted as a burgess of Dumfries in 1750. [DBR]

BROOM, WILLIAM, a baxter, was admitted as a burgess of Dumfries in 1757. [DBR]

BROWN, CUTHBERT, residing in Dumfries, suspected of Catholicism, 1601. [RPCS.VI.312]

BROWN, GEORGE, in Moss-side, parish of Dumfries, testament, 1683, Comm. Dumfries. [NRS]

BROWN, ISABEL, spouse of John Carlyle a merchant burgess of Dumfries, testament, 1629, Comm. Dumfris. [NRS]

BROWN, JOHN, at the Bridgend of Dumfries, 1621. [RPCS.XII. 586]

BROWN, JOHN, a bailie of Dumfries, testament [missing] 1694, Comm. Dumfries. [NRS]

BROWN, JOHN, a merchant in Dumfries, deeds, 1702, [NRS.RD3.99.2.289; RD4.91.412]; sasines, 1707/1710/1718. [NRS.RS23.7/224/469; 9/150]; testaments [missing] 1703, 1705, 1707, Comm. Dumfries. [NRS]

BROWN, JOHN, treasurer of Dumfries, testament [missing 1709, 1710, Comm. Dumfries. [NRS]

BROWN, JOHN, a weaver, was admitted as a burgess of Dumfries in 1750. [DBR]

BROWN, MARGARET, in Dumfries, daughter of John Brown of Nunland, and relict of Hugh Cairns of Lochill, sasines, 1716-1728. [NRS.RS23.10/215, 220, 311, 393]

BROWN, PATRICK, a merchant in Dumfries, 1622. [NAS.E71.10.5]

BROWN, RICHARD, educated at Glasgow University, graduated MA in 1649, minister of St Michael's, Dumfries, from 1685 until 1690, died in Edinburgh 1707. [F.2.265]

BROWN, ROBERT, a merchant in Dumfries, 1698. [NRS.RH8.260.1]; a deed, 1702, [NRS.RD4.91.412]; sasines, 1703. [NRS.RS23.387-388]

BROWN, THOMAS, a merchant in Dumfries, a sasine, 22 May 1707. [NRS.RS23.7.224]

BROWN, WILLIAM, a merchant in Dumfries, 1621. [NAS.E71.10.5]

BROWN, WILLIAM, a watchmaker, was admitted as a burgess of Dumfries in 1753. [DBR]; a clock-maker in Dumfries, died 14 November 1795. [OSC.66]

BRYAN, JAMES, a merchant in Dumfries, testament, 1776, Comm. Dumfries, [NRS]

BRYCE, JOHN, the younger, residing in Dumfries, suspected of Catholicism, 1601. [RPCS.VI.312]

BRYCE, JOHN, residing in Dumfries, suspected of Catholicism, 1601. [RPCS.VI.312]

BRYDEN, JOHN, an innkeeper, was admitted as a burgess of Dumfries in 1740. [DBR]

BRYDEN, JOHN, a tailor, was admitted as a burgess of Dumfries in 1750. [DBR]

BRYDEN, JOSEPH, a flax-dresser, was admitted as a burgess of Dumfries in 1799. [DBR]

BRYDEN, THOMAS, a merchant, was admitted as a burgess of Dumfries in 1744. [DBR]

BRYDEN, WILLIAM, a tobacconist in Dumfries, 1786. [NRS.CE51.Letterbook]

BURGESS, JAMES, a merchant burgess of Dumfries, testament, 1639, Comm. Dumfries. [NRS]

BURGESS, JAMES, a baker, was admitted as a burgess of Dumfries in 1799. [DBR]

BURGESS, JANET, daughter of Herbert Burgess in Woodneuck, and spouse of James Lindsay a wigmaker in Dumfries, a sasine, 8 August 1723. [NRS.RS23.10.72]

BURGESS, JOHN, a merchant, was admitted as a burgess of Dumfries in 1740. [DBR]

BURGESS, ROBERT, a merchant, was admitted as a burgess of Dumfries in 1756. [DBR]; testament, 1775, Comm. Dumfries. [NRS]

BURGESS, WILLIAM, a flax-dresser, was admitted as a burgess of Dumfries in 1771. [DBR]

BURNS, ROBERT, born 1759, settled in Dumfries 1791, died there on 21 July 1796. [St Michael's MI]; an Excise officer in Dumfries, testament, 1796, Comm. Dumfries. [NRS]

BURNSIDE, JAMES, born 18 April 1788 in Dumfries, son of Reverend William Burnside and his wife Ann Hutton, died 1815 in India. [F.2.267][St Michael's, Dumfries, MI]

BURNSIDE, WILLIAM, born 1751, son of William Burnside in Glasgow, graduated MA from Glasgow University in 1769, minister in Dumfries, from 1780 until hs death 5 January 1806. Husband of Ann Hutton, parents of Margaret who married William Walker in Jamaica, Janet, Mary, Ann, William, Helen, James who died in India, and Jane. [F.2.267]

BUSHBIE, JOHN, an innkeeper, was admitted as a burgess of Dumfries in 1755. [DBR]

BUTTERWELL, ABRAHAM, a weaver, was admitted as a burgess of Dumfries in 1739. [DBR]

CAIG, ANDREW, a slater, was admitted as a burgess of Dumfries, 1759. [DBR]

CAIG, ROBERT, a slater and joiner, was admitted as a burgess of Dumfries, 1759.   [DBR]

CAIRD, HERBERT, a merchant in Dumfries, relict Bessie
Blackstock, testament, 1674, Comm. Dumfries. [NRS]

CAIRD, JOHN, was admitted as a burgess of Dumfries in 1664. [DBR]; a
merchant in Dumfries, testament, 1674, Comm. Dumfries. [NRS]

CAIRD, JOHN, a smith, was admitted as a burgess of Dumfries, 1759. [DBR]

CAIRMONT, WILLIAM, was admitted as a burgess of Dumfries in 1678.
[DBR]; a merchant in Dumfries, 1707. [NRS.CS228.B1.42]

CAIRNCROSS, ALEXANDER, MA, minister of St Michael's,
Dumfries, from 1668 until 1684. [F.2.265]

CALDER, JOHN, was admitted as a burgess of Dumfries in 1656. [DBR]; a
weaver in Dumfries, testament, 1688, Comm. Dumfries. [NRS]

CALLENDAR, JAMES, a tobacconist, was admitted as a burgess of Dumfries,
1757. [DBR]

CALVERT, JOHN, a merchant in Dumfries, 1621. [NRS.E71.10.5]

CAMPBELL, GEORGE, MA, minister of St Michael's, Dumfries,
from 1658 to 1662, and from 1687 until 1690. [F.2.265]

CAMPBELL, SAMUEL, master of the Marion of Dumfries, 1689.
[NRS.E72.6.13]

CANNON, JOHN, was admitted as a burgess of Dumfries in 1705. [DBR]; a
merchant in Dumfries, 1708. [NRS.AC9.313]

CAPLES, JAMES, in Dumfries, 1687. [RPCS.XIII.172]

CARLISLE, AGNES, MARGARET, and JANET, heirs to their
father William Carlisle, a bailie burgess of Dumfries, 1658.
[NRS.Retours, Dumfries, 235]

CARLYLE, AGNES, relict of James Veitch a merchant in
Dumfries, testament, 1729, Comm. Dumfries. [NRS]

CARLYLE, ALEXANDER, a merchant from Dumfries, settled in
Hopewell, Somerset County, Maryland, by 1712, died 1726.
[MSA.MdProv.Ct.12/127; WMQ.1.18.206]

CARLYLE, GAVIN, was admitted as a burgess of Dumfries in 1670. [DBR]; a merchant in Dumfries, a deed, 1699, [NRS.RD2/82.269]; husband of Agnes Hood, a sasine 1719. [NRS.RS23.9.226]

CARLYLE, ISOBEL, a Roman Catholic in Dumfries, 1704. [NRS.CH1.5.2]

CARLYLE, ISOBEL, spouse of Herbert Irving a merchant burgess of Dumfries, testament, 1661, Comm. Dumfries. [NRS]

CARLISLE, JAMES, a merchant in Dumfries, 1677. [NRS.AC7.4]

CARLYLE, JANET, spouse of John Broache a merchant in Dumfries, testament, 1680, Comm. Dumfries. [NRS]

CARLISLE, JOHN, a merchant burgess of Dumfries, 1622, [NRS.E71.10.5]; his spouse Isobel Brown, testament, 1629, Comm. Dumfries. [NRS]

CARLISLE, JOHN, a workman burgess in Dumfries, testament, 1681, Comm. Dumfries. [NRS]

CARLISLE, JOHN, master of the Margaret of Dumfries, 1688-1691. [NRS.E72.6.13/18/24/25]

CARLYLE, JOHN, born 1720, son of Alexander Carlyle, a merchant from Dumfries, settled in Alexandria, Virginia, by 1748, died 1780. [NRS.SC36.63.1; RS10.16.31][VaGaz.837/852]

CARLYLE, THOMAS, a writer, was admitted as a burgess of Dumfries, 1761. [DBR]; testament 1778, Comm. Dumfries. [NRS]

CARLISLE, WILLIAM, a merchant in Dumfries, trading with Flanders, 1622. [NRS.E71.10.5]; a merchant bailie of Dumfries, a deed, 1645. [NRS.GD219.147]

CARLISLE, WILLIAM, late bailie of Dumfries, testament, 1659, Comm. Dumfries. [NRS]

CARMICHAEL, ROBERT, a Customs officer at Dumfries, 1784. [NRS.CE51.2/3]

CARMONT, JOHN, was admitted as a burgess of Dumfries in 1671. [DBR]; a workman in Dumfries, testament, 1686, Comm. Dumfries. [NRS]

CARNOCHAN, JOHN, born 1778 in Dumfries, emigrated to Nassau, later settled in Georgia, husband of Harriet F. Putnam, father of John Murray Carnochan, [1812-1841]. [BLG.2602]

CARRAN, ROBERT, residing in Dumfries, suspected of Catholicism, 1601. [RPCS.VI.312]

CARRUTHERS, FRANCIS, a joiner, was admitted as a burgess of Dumfries, 1771. [DBR]

CARRUTHERS, JAMES, born 1744, died 28 March 1784. [St Michael's MI, Dumfries]

CARRUTHERS, JAMES, of Warmanbie, a resident of Dumfries, testament, 1798, Comm. Dumfries. [NRS]

CARRUTHERS, JAMES, born in Dumfries, a merchant in Savannah, Georgia, died 9 September 1820 in Augusta, Georgia. [Colonial Museum; and Savannah Advertiser, 19.9.1820]

CARRUTHERS, JOHN, a joiner, was admitted as a burgess of Dumfries, 1765. [DBR]

CARRUTHERS, LANS, a tailor, was admitted as a burgess of Dumfries, 1742. [DBR]

CARRUTHERS, THOMAS, son of John Carruthers a joiner, [1734-1823], and his wife Anne Haining, died aged 23 in Jamaica. [Dumfries MI]

CARRUTHERS, WILLIAM, a merchant, was admitted as a burgess of Dumfries, 1740. [DBR]; a merchant in Dumfries, and Robert Kennan, a merchant in Virginia, versus Jean Kennan, wife of John Wallace, a merchant in Dumfries, 25 February 1769. [NRA.CS16.1.134]; a letter 1746. [NRS.GD18.5738]; letters, 1755-1753. [NRS.GD18.1164-1173]

CARSAN, JOHN, was admitted as a burgess of Dumfries in 1695. [DBR]; a merchant in Dumfries, and his wife Margaret Maxwell, a sasine, 14 November 1704. [NRS.RS23.7.60]

CARSAN, JOHN, a merchant, was admitted as a burgess of Dumfries, 1755. [DBR]

CARTER, JAMES, an innkeeper, was admitted as a burgess of Dumfries, 1798. [DBR]

CARTER, ROBERT, residing in Dumfries, suspected of Catholicism, 1601. [RPCS.VI.312]

CHALMERS, JAMES, MA, minister of St Michael's, Dumfries from 1662 to 1667. [F.2.265]

CHALMERS, JOHN, was admitted as a burgess of Dumfries in 1674. [DBR]; a merchant in Dumfries, trading with Danzig, 1713. [NRS.AC9.443]

CHALMERS, ROBERT, a merchant, was admitted as a burgess of Dumfries, 1756. [DBR]

CHARTERS, AGNES, spouse of John Rae, in Dumfries, testament, 1742, Comm. Dumfries. [NRS]

CHARTERS, JAMES, a merchant in Dumfries, a bond, 1648. [NRS.GD42.D17]

CHARTERS, JANET, relict of James McAnce a merchant burgess of Dumfries, testament, 1678, Comm. Dumfris. [NRS]

CHARTERS, JOHN, a shopkeeper, was admitted as a burgess of Dumfries, 1751. [DBR]

CHARTERS, WILLIAM, in Dumfries, testament, 1788, Comm. Dumfries. [NRS]

CHIESLY, BARBARA, spouse of John Johnstone a merchant in Dumfries, testament, 1680, Comm.Dumfries. [NRS]

CHRISTIE, ALEXANDER, was admitted as a burgess of Dumfries in 1688. [DBR]; a wine-cooper in Dumfries, sasines, 1711/1721. [NRS.RS23.8/46; 9/311]

CHRISTIE, GEORGE, a baker, was admitted as a burgess of Dumfries, 1769. [DBR]

CHRISTIE, JOHN, a goldsmith, was admitted as a burgess of Dumfries, 1755. [DBR]

CHURRIE, WILLIAM, in Burnfoot, Dumfries, testament, 1638, Comm. Dumfries. [NRS]

CLARK, ADAM, Ormond Pursuivant, a burgess of Dumfries, testament, 1641, Comm. Dumfries. [NRS]

CLARK, DAVID, in Whitehills of Craig, parish of Dumfries, testament, 1793, Comm. Dumfries. [NRS]

CLARK, JAMES, born 1707, a bailie of Dumfries, died 27 December 1783, husband of Mary Costine. [St Michael's MI]

CLARK, JAMES, a merchant, was admitted as a burgess of Dumfries, 1739. [DBR]

CLARK, JAMES, a barber in Dumfries, testament, 1644, Comm. Dumfries. [NRS]

CLARK, JOHN, baron of the Exchequer of Scotland, was admitted as a burgess of Dumfries, 1708. [NRS.GD18.2052]

CLARK, JOHN, a writer, was admitted as a burgess of Dumfries, 1744. [DBR]

CLARK, JOHN, born 1779, son of ...... Clark and his wife Margaret Scott, settled in Louisiana, died 9 April 1866 in Maxwelltown. [Dumfries MI]

CLARK, JOHN, of the George Inn, Dumfries, 1797. [NRS.CS97.102.18]; testaments, 1800/1801, Comm. Dumfries. [NRS]

CLARK, SAMUEL, a schoolmaster, was admitted as a burgess of Dumfries, 1744. [DBR]

CLARK, SAMUEL, a writer in Dumfries, and his son Samuel Clark the Commissary there, papers, 1749-1808. [NRS.CC5.21.4]; a writer, was admitted as a burgess of Dumfries, 1759. [DBR]

CLARK, WILLIAM, born 1668, a bailie of Dumfries, died 4 April 1751, husband of Elizabeth Callander. [St Michael's MI]

CLARK, WILLIAM, born 1711, a writer, died 19 April 1783, testaments, 1785, 1786, 1793, Comm. Dumfries, [NRS]; husband of Janet Costine, their son William Clark, also a writer, died 26 January 1783. [St Michael's MI]; a writer, was admitted as a burgess of Dumfries, 1750. [DBR]

CLARK, WILLIAM, a merchant, was admitted as a burgess of Dumfries, 1752. [DBR]

CLARK and NEWALL, in Dumfries, letters, 1755-1756. [NRS.RH15.66.3]

CLEUGH, WILLIAM, a tidewaiter at Dumfries, testament, 1778, Comm. Dumfries. [NRS]

CLINT, HENRY, was admitted as a burgess of Dumfries in 1790, [DBR]; a writer in Dumfries, 1799. [NRS.CS97.112.119]

COLLINS, SAMUEL, master of the brig Edington of Dumfries in 1770s. [PA. 26]

COLTART, JOHN, was admitted as a burgess of Dumfries in 1673, [DBR]; a weaver in Dumfries, and his relict Catherine Donaldson, sasines, 1710/1722/1727. [NRS.RS23.7/467; 10/10.287]

COLTART, JOHN, of Areling, a writer in Dumfries, versus William Turner, sailor in North Carolina, eldest son of John Turner of Ardwell, 1765; 1773. [NRS.CS16.1.120; CS229.C3.44]

COLTART, NICHOL, a Customs officer at Dumfries, 1784. [NRS.CE51.2/3]

COLTART, ROBERT, master of the John and Robert of Dumfries trading with Gothenborg, Sweden, in 1754. [NRS.E504.9.2]

COLVIN, ANDREW, a shoemaker, was admitted as a burgess of Dumfries, 1768. [DBR]

COPLAND, ALEXANDER, a surgeon, was admitted as a burgess of Dumfries in 1775 [DBR]; a surgeon in Dumfries, 1780. [NRS.CS228.B.6.46]

COPLAND, JAMES, a merchant burgess of Dumfries, 1600. [RPCS.VI.636]

COPLAND, JOHN, Provost of Dumfries, 1683, [RPCS.VIII.132]; testaments, 1687-1688, Comm. Dumfries. [NRS]; born 1617, died February 1695. [St Michael's MI]

COPLAND, WILLIAM, heir to his father John Copland the Provost of Dumfries, 1687. [NRS.Retours, Dumfries, 318]

COPLAND, of Colliston, WILLIAM, former Provost of Dumfries, sasines, 1708-1732. [NRS.RS23.6.116, etc][EUL.LC.3036]

COPLAND, of Colliston, WILLIAM, born 1638, died 9 February 1715, husband of Anne, daughter of Sir Thomas Gordon of Earlston, parents of Alexander Copland, born 1700, died 11 June 1774, Thomas Copland of Blackwood, an advocate, born 1707, died 2 September 1735, and Susan Copland.. [St Michael's MI, Dumfries]

CORBET, ADAM, was admitted as a burgess of Dumfries in 1655, [DBR]; a merchant burgess of Dumfries, testament, 1659, Comm. Dumfries. [NRS]

CORBETT, JAMES, master of the Unity of Dumfries arrived at Hampton, Virginia, 16 May 1738. [TNA.CO5.1320]; a merchant and ship-owner in Dumfries, records, 1748-1756. [NRS.CS96.2147-2162]; trading with Virginia, 1737-1762. [DGA.Misc.RB2.2.169][NRS.CS96.2147-2162; E504.9.1/2]

CORBETT, JAMES, a merchant, was admitted as a burgess of Dumfries, 1749. [DBR]

CORBETT, JOHN, a merchant burgess of Dumfries, testament, 1630, Comm. Dumfries. [NRS]

CORBETT, JOHN, born 1630, bailie of Dumfries, died 20 November 1682. [St Michael's MI, Dumfries]

CORBETT, JOHN, in Dumfries, 1715. [NRS.E669.10]

CORBETT, JOHN, former merchant bailie and Provost of Dumfries, sasines, 1704-1724. [NRS.RS23, 7/296, etc]

CORBET, ROBERT, a merchant bailie and Provost of Dumfries, sasines, 1708-1730. [NRS.RS23.7/296; 10/44, 476]

CORBETT, THOMAS, a merchant in Dumfries, trading with Virginia, 1745-1753. [NRS.CS96.2156-2162; E504.9.2]; was admitted as a burgess of Dumfries, 1754. [DBR]

CORBETT, WILLIAM, in Dumfries, letters, 1680. [NRS.RH15.106.374]

CORBETT, WILLIAM, a merchant in Dumfries, a sasine, 21 July 1730. [NRS.RS23.11.18]

CORBETT, WILLIAM, Customs Controller at Dumfries, 1743. [NRS.E504.9.1]

CORRIE, ARCHIBALD, a merchant in Bath and Edenton, North Carolina, eldest son of James Corrie of Spedden, Provost of Dumfries, 17 November 1770. [NRS.CS16.1.143]

CORRIE, EDWARD, a merchant, was admitted as a burgess of Dumfries, 1746. [DBR]

CORRIE, HUGH, factor for Alexander Johnston, Hugh Lawson, and Company, bankers in Dumfries, versus Joseph Corrie in Dominica, 1782. [NRS.CS17.1.1]

CORRIE, WILLIAM, a merchant, was admitted as a burgess of Dumfries, 1741. [DBR]

CORSANE, ADAM, residing in Dumfries, suspected of Catholicism, 1601. [RPCS.VI.312]

CORSAN, JOHN, residing in Dumfries, suspected of Catholicism, 1601. [RPCS.VI.312]; a bailie burgess of Dumfries, accused of liberating a prisoner from Dumfries Prison, 1600. [RPCS.VI.636]

CORSAN, JOHN, Provost of Dumfries, 1619. [RPCS.XII.98]; died 7 May 1629, [St Michael's MI]; testament, 1643, Comm. Dumfries. [NRS]

CORSANE, ROBERT, of Meikleknox, born 1698, died 17 February 1759; husband of Agnes McGowne, parents of Janet, spouse of David McCulloch of Ardwall, born 1740, died 16 March 1824 in Dumfries. [St Michael's MI]

CORSANE, WILLIAM, a shopkeeper, was admitted as a burgess of Dumfries, 1757. [DBR]

CORSBIE, ANDREW, a merchant burgess of Dumfries, testament, 1674, Comm. Dumfries. [NRS]

CORSBIE, ISABEL, spouse of Robert Paterson a merchant burgess of Dumfries, testament, 1625, Comm. Dumfries. [NRS]

CORSBIE, WILLIAM, a shoemaker at Bridgend, Dumfries, testament, 1686. Comm. Dumfries. [NRS]

COSTAN, HUGH, a merchant in Dumfries, trading with Flanders, 1622. [NRS.E71.10.5]; a merchant burgess of Dumfries, testament, 1639, Comm. Dumfries. [NRS]

COURTAS, JOHN, was admitted as a burgess of Dumfries in 1778, [DBR]; a merchant in Dumfries, 1786. [NRS.CE51.Letterbook]

COWAN, BARBARA, a Covenanter imprisoned in Dumfries Tolbooth, transported to East New Jersey in 1685. [RPCS.XI.291]

COWAN, BENJAMIN, an innkeeper, was admitted as a burgess of Dumfries, 1740. [DBR]

COWAN, HOMER, a workman, was admitted as a burgess of Dumfries, 1762. [DBR]

COWAN, JAMES, an innkeeper in Dumfries, testament, 1761, Comm. Dumfries. [NRS]

COWAN, JOHN, a weaver, was admitted as a burgess of Dumfries, 1739. [DBR]

COWPAR, ROBERT, a mason burgess of Dumfries, 1601. [RPCS.VI.263]Willi

CRAIK, ADAM, was admitted as a burgess of Dumfries in 1721, [DBR]; a merchant in Dumfries, 1727. [NRS.AC9.1037]

CRAIK, ELIZABETH, widow of Thomas Irving, Provost of Dumfries, testament, 1732, Comm. Dumfries. [NRS]

CRAIK, JAMES, of Stewarton, heir to his father John Craik a merchant bailie of Dumfries, [NRS.Retours, Dumfries, 177]; testament, 1687, Comm. Dumfries. [NRS]

CRAIK, JOHN, a merchant in Dumfries, trading with Flanders, 1622. [NRS.E71.10.5]; a deed, 1629. [NRS.GD28.1348]

CRAIK, MARION, daughter of William Craik, and relict of James Maxwell a notary in Dumfries, a deed, 1702. [NRS.RD4.91.178]

CRAIK, ROBERT, a mason, was admitted as a burgess of Dumfries, 1750. [DBR]

CRAIK, WILLIAM, of Arbigland, Provost of Dumfries, died 1 April 1697. [St Michael's MI]; Provost in 1683, accused of allowing a prisoner to escape from Dumfries Tolbooth. [RPCS.VIII.152]

CRAIK, WILLIAM, in Parkfoot, Dumfries, testament, 1775, Comm. Dumfries. [NRS]

CRAW, WILLIAM, a silver-smith, was admitted as a burgess of Dumfries, 1769. [DBR]

CRAWFORD, SAMUEL, a chaise driver in Dumfries, testament, 1793, Comm. Dumfries. [NRS]

CREIGHTON, THOMAS, was admitted as a burgess of Dumfries, 1759. [DBR]

CRICHTON, ELIZABETH, daughter of Robert Crichton of Ryhill, and spouse of John Irving the younger, a bailie in Dumfries, a sasine, 25 December 1729. [NRS.RS23.10.480]

CRICHTOUN, JAMES, of St Leonards, Sheriff of Dumfries, a decree, 1666. [NRS.GD1.403.28]

CROCKETT, GILBERT, was admitted as a burgess of Dumfries in 1675, [DBR]; a merchant in Dumfries, spouse Marion Blacklock, testaments, 1687, 1693, Comm. Dumfries; relict Mary, daughter of John McMichan, daughter of John McMichan of Barcaple, a deed, 1696. [NRS.RD2.79.795]

CROCKETT, JAMES, a baxter, was admitted as a burgess of Dumfries, 1750. [DBR]

CROCKETT, JOHN, a burgess of Dumfries, accused of liberating a prisoner from Dumfries Prison, 1600. [RPCS.VI.636]

CROCKETT, JOHN, a merchant in Dumfries, spouse Mary Newlands, a deed, 1699. [NRS.RD4.85.87]; testaments, 1722, 1723, 1731, Comm. Dumfries. [NRS]

CROCKETT, JOHN, a dyer, was admitted as a burgess of Dumfries, 1740. [DBR]

CROCKETT, MARY, in Dumfries, widow of John Newall a farmer in Auchencairn, testament, 1792, Comm. Dumfries. [NRS]

CROCKETT, ROBERT, a baxter, was admitted as a burgess of Dumfries, 1744. [DBR]; testament, 1749, Comm. Dumfries. [NRS]

CROCKETT, WILLIAM, a merchant in Dumfries, a deed, 1710. [NRS.GD219.207]; testament, 1744, Comm. Dumfries. [NRS]

CROCKETT, WILLIAM, a wright, was admitted as a burgess of Dumfries, 1744. [DBR]

CROMBIE, ALEXANDER, a mason, was admitted as a burgess of Dumfries, 1747. [DBR]

CROMBIE, PETER, a mason, was admitted as a burgess of Dumfries, 1769. [DBR]

CROSBIE, ANDREW, was admitted as a burgess of Dumfries in 1701, [DBR]; a merchant in Dumfries, 1703/1706, [NRS.AC9.18; AC13.1.53]; owner of the Kirkconnell, master William Johnston, 1721. [NRS.AC9.764]; ref in charter of 1707. [EUL.LC3036]

CROSBIE, ANDREW, a merchant in Dumfries, trading with Virginia, 1746. 1750, [NRS.E504.9.1/2]

CROSBIE, JAMES, a saddler, was admitted as a burgess of Dumfries, 1741. [DBR]

CROSBIE, JAMES, was admitted as a burgess of Dumfries in 1776, [DBR]; a tobacconist in Dumfries, 1786. [NRS.CE51.Letterbook]

CROSBIE, JOHN, of Holm, born 1651, a merchant and Provost of Dumfries, died 12 July 1720. [St Michael's MI]; a merchant bailie of Dumfries, a charter 1707. [EUL.LC.3036]; was appointed a trade convenor of Dumfries in 1686 by King James VII. [RPCS.XIII.43]

CROSBIE, JOHN, a sailor in Dumfries, testament, 1746, Comm. Dumfries. [NSR]

CROSBIE, JOHN, a tobacconist, was admitted as a burgess of Dumfries, 1747. [DBR]

CROSBIE, JOHN, a merchant, was admitted as a burgess of Dumfries, 1752. [DBR]

CROSBIE, JOHN, a merchant, was admitted as a burgess of Dumfries, 1797. [DBR]

CROSBIE, THOMAS, was admitted as a burgess of Dumfries in 1786, [DBR]; a tobacconist in Dumfries, 1786. [NRS.CE51.Letterbook]

CROSBIE, WILLIAM, a tailor, was admitted as a burgess of Dumfries, 1750. [DBR]; Convenor of the Trades of Dumfries, testament, 1776, Comm. Dumfries. [NRS]

CROSBIE, WILLIAM, a wright, was admitted as a burgess of Dumfries, 1750. [DBR]

CROSBIE, WILLIAM, a shopkeeper, was admitted as a burgess of Dumfries, 1767. [DBR]

CUMING, SAMUEL, a tailor, was admitted as a burgess of Dumfries, 1741. [DBR]

CUNNINGHAM, CATHERINE, spouse of Thomas McMullan a merchant burgess of Dumfries, testament, 1627, Comm. Dumfries. [NRS]

CUNNINGHAM, CUTHBERT, a bailie burgess, residing in Dumfries, suspected of Catholicism, 1601. [RPCS.VI.312];

CUNNINGHAM, HERBERT, a burgess of Dumfries, and sheriff-depute, a sasine, 1603. [NRS.GD136.1.257]

CUNNINGHAM, JAMES, a tailor, was admitted as a burgess of Dumfries, 1747.   [DBR]

CUNNINGHAM, JANET, relict of John Corbet a bailie of Dumfries, sasine, 23 April 1708. [NRS.RS23.7.296]

CUNNINGHAM, JOHN, a merchant in Dumfries, testaments, 1723, 1745, Comm. Dumfries. [NRS]

CUNNINGHAM, JOHN, a merchant in Dumfries, testament, 1772, Comm. Dumfries. [NRS]

CUNNINGHAM, MARION, spouse of James Aitken, merchant at the Bridgend of Dumfries, sasine, 27 February 1703. [NRS.RS6.398]

CUNNINGHAM, ROBERT, a burgess, residing in Dumfries, suspected of Catholicism, 1601. [RPCS.VI.312]

CUNNINGHAM ROBERT, a notary in Dumfries, testament, 1608, Comm. Edinburgh. [NRS]

CUNNINGHAM, ROBERT, a merchant, was admitted as a burgess of Dumfries, 1739. [DBR]

CUNNINGHAM, WILLIAM, a tailor, was admitted as a burgess of Dumfries, 1764. [DBR]

CURRIE, DAVID, son of William Currie in Dumfries, 1793. [NRS.CS97.110.94]

CURRIE, JAMES, former Provost of Dumfries, 1728. [NRS.AC9.989]

CURRIE, JOSEPH, a writer in Dumfries, son of William Currie a merchant bailie of Dumfries, a deed, 1715, [NRS.RD3.145.399]; factory papers, 1727-1738. [NRS.GD18.2585]

CURROW, WILLIAM, a merchant in Dumfries, testament, 1686, Comm. Dumfries. [NRS]

CUTLER, ROBERT, son of Archibald Cutler of Orraland, a merchant in Dumfries, was admitted a burgess of Dumfries, 1731. [NRS.GD77.196.5][DBR]

DALGLEISH, JAMES, born 1695, died 9 May 1733. [St Michael's MI]; was admitted as a burgess of Dumfries in 1728. [DBR]; testament, 1728, Comm. Dumfries. [NRS]

DALRYMPLE, DANIEL, was admitted as a burgess of Dumfries in 1707, [DBR]; a pewterer in Dumfries, a deed, 1715. [NRS.RD2.104.958]

DALTON, JOSEPH, a hucker, was admitted as a burgess of Dumfries, 1768. [DBR]

DALZELL, ARCHIBALD, a tobacconist in Dumfries, 1786. [NRS.CE51.Letterbook]; was admitted as a burgess of Dumfries in 1773, [DBR];

DALZIEL, WILLIAM and ROBERT, merchants in Dumfries, records 1770-1771. [NRS.CS96.49.50]

DAMSTER, ROBERT, a carter, was admitted as a burgess of Dumfries, 1750. [DBR]

DARGARVEL, CHARLES, a gardener, was admitted as a burgess of Dumfries, 1752. [DBR]

DAVIDSON, ISOBEL, daughter of Andrew Davidson a merchant in Dumfries, testament, 1765, Comm. Dumfries. [NRS]

DAVIDSON, JOHN, at the Bridgend of Dumfries, testament, 1757, Comm. Dumfries. [NRS]

DAVIDSON, MARGARET, spouse of James Bartan a merchant burgess of Dumfries, testament, 1638, Comm. Dumfries. [NRS]

DAVIDSON, THOMAS, an innkeeper in Dumfries, testament, 1755, Comm. Dumfries. [NRS]

DENUNE, WILLIAM, a painter in Dumfries, testament, 1755, Comm. Dumfries. [NRS]

DICK, ALEXANDER, a minister, was admitted as a burgess of Dumfries, 1747. [DBR]

DICKSON, ADAM, a barber burgess of Dumfries, testament, 1678, Comm. Dumfries. [NRS]

DICKSON, ALEXANDER, was admitted as a burgess of Dumfries in 1784, [DBR]; a tobacconist in Dumfries, 1786. [NRS.CE51.Letterbook]; testaments, 1791, 1792, Comm.Dumfries. [NRS]

DICKSON, GEORGE, a merchant in Dumfries, testament, 1680, Comm. Dumfries. [NRS]

DICKSON, HARBERT, a burgess of Dumfries, was accused of liberating a prisoner from Dumfries Prison, 1600. [RPCS.VI.636]

DICKSON, HENRY, an innkeeper, was admitted as a burgess of Dumfries, 1767. [DBR]

DICKSON, JAMES, a writer, was admitted as a burgess of Dumfries, 1742 [DBR]

DICKSON, JOHN, a merchant in Dumfries, 1621. [NRS.E71.10.5]

DICKSON, JOHN, a merchant, was admitted as a burgess of Dumfries, 1740. [DBR]

DICKSON, JOSEPH, a merchant, was admitted as a burgess of Dumfries, 1754. [DBR]

DICKSON, JOSEPH, a Customs officer at Dumfries, 1784. [NRS.CE51.2/3]

DICKSON, MARK, a burgess in Dumfries, testament, 1730, Comm. Dumfries. [NRS]

DICKSON, MARY, daughter of John Dickson the Convenor of Trades in Dumfries, and his wife Helen Bell, widow of Bruce Bell a vintner in Dumfries, testament, 1776, Comm. Dumfries. [NRS]

DICKSON, NICHOLAS, a tanner, was admitted as a burgess of Dumfries, 1750. [DBR]

DICKSON, RICHARD. a baxter, was admitted as a burgess of Dumfries, 1742. [DBR]

DICKSON, THOMAS, a baxter, was admitted as a burgess of Dumfries, 1754. [DBR]

DICKSON, WILLIAM, a staymaker, was admitted as a burgess of Dumfries, 1749. [DBR]

DINGWALL, MATTHEW, dancing master in Dumfries, testament, 1786, Comm. Dumfries. [NRS]

DINNISTON, JAMES, a merchant, was admitted as a burgess of Dumfries, 1798. [DBR]

DINWIDDIE, JAMES, a dealer, was admitted as a burgess of Dumfries, 1799. [DBR]

DINWIDDIE, MARY, widow of James Gibson the Deacon of the Fleshers of Dumfries, testament, 1791, Comm. Dumfries. [NRS]

DOBIE, JOHN, a musician in Dumfries, testament, 1759, Comm.Dumfries. [NRS]

DODDS, JAMES, was admitted as a burgess of Dumfries in 1706, [DBR]; a merchant in Dumfries, 1727. [NRS.AC8.353]; testament, 1778, Comm. Dumfries. [NRS]

DODD, WILLIAM, a merchant, was admitted as a burgess of Dumfries, 1740'
[DBR]

DONALD, ROBERT, a merchant, was admitted as a burgess of Dumfries, 1757.
[DBR]

DONALDSON, EBENEZER, a surgeon in Dumfries, testament, 1786, Comm.
Dumfries. [NRS]

DONALDSON, JOSEPH, a merchant, was admitted as a burgess of Dumfries,
1737. [DBR]

DONALDSON, ROBERT, born 4 March 1764 in Barnkiss, Dumfries, son of
John Donaldson and his wife Margaret Tait, married Sarah Henderson in North
Carolina 26 March 1795, a merchant in New York, died in Brunswick County,
North Carolina, on 8 July 1808. [ANY.I.391]

DOUGLAS, ALEXANDER, a baxter, was admitted as a burgess of Dumfries,
1753. [DBR]

DOUGLAS, ALEXANDER, a barber, was admitted as a burgess of Dumfries,
1766. [DBR]

DOUGLAS, DAVID, a barber, was admitted as a burgess of Dumfries, 1743.
[DBR]

DOUGLAS, DAVID, a Customs officer at Dumfries, 1784. [NRS.CE51.2/3];
testaments, 1793, 1794, 1801, Comm. Dumfries. [NRS]

DOUGLAS, HENRY, a dyer in Dumfries, testament, 1730, Comm. Dumfries,
[NRS]

DOUGLAS, JAMES, a stabler burgess of Dumfries, testament, 1684, Comm.
Dumfries. [NRS]

DOUGLAS, JAMES, of Mouswald, residing in Dumfries, testament, 1684,
Comm. Dumfries. [NRS]

DRINNAN, ROBERT, a sailor aboard the Mally of Dumfries which was
captured by an American privateer when bound for Nova Scotia in 1776 but was
later liberated by the Royal Navy in 1777. [NRS.AC7.60]

DRONNAN, HELEN, servant of Jean Glencorse a widow in Dumfries, 1687.
[RPCS.XIII.169]

DUFF, HOMER, was admitted as a burgess of Dumfries in 1701, [DBR]; a shopkeeper in Dumfries, 1707. [NRS.AC9.246]

DUFF, JOHN, a workman, was admitted as a burgess of Dumfries in 1701, [DBR]; a merchant in Dumfries, 1707. [EUL.LC3036]

DUFF, ROBERT, a tailor, was admitted as a burgess of Dumfries, 1762. [DBR]

DUN, JAMES, a weaver, was admitted as a burgess of Dumfries, 1764. [DBR]

DUNBAR, DAVID, son of Thomas Dunbar, late dean in Dumfries, a witness, 1687. [RPCS.XIII.156]

DUNBAR, GAVIN, a merchant burgess of Dumfries, and his wife Margaret Young, testaments, 1731, 1733, Comm. Dumfries. [NRS]

DUNBAR, MARGARET, arrived in Dumfries from Ireland in 1690. [NRS.CH2.537.15.1/34]

DUNBAR, THOMAS, Dean of Guild in Dumfries, 1683. [RPCS.VIII.152]

DUNCAN, EDWARD, a carter, was admitted as a burgess of Dumfries, 1765. [DBR]

DUNCAN and WATSON, merchants in Dumfries, 1797. [NRS.97.112.68]

DUNLOP, JOHN, joiner, was admitted as a burgess of Dumfries, 1761. [DBR]

DUNLOP, JOHN, a tobacconist in Dumfries, 1786. [NRS.CE51.Letterbook]

DURNISTON, JOHN, a dyer, was admitted as a burgess of Dumfries, 1765. [DBR]

EASON, ROBERT, master of the Countess of Dumfries, bound for South Carolina, October 1774. [TNA.T47.12]

EDGAR, AGNES, daughter of Edward Edgar a merchant in Dumfries, testament, 1685, Comm. Dumfries. [NRS]

EDGAR, DAVID, was admitted as a burgess of Dumfries in 1647, [DBR]; a merchant burgess of Dumfries, testament, 1676, Comm. Dumfries. [NRS]

EDGAR, EDWARD, a merchant burgess of Dumfries, testament, 1679, Comm. Dumfries. [NRS]

EDGAR, ISOBEL, spouse of Matthew Rowie a burgess of Dumfries, testament, 1629, Comm. Dumfries. [NRS]

EDGAR, ISOBEL, spouse of Thomas Aikin a cordiner in Dumfries, testament, 1689, Comm. Dumfries. [NRS]

EDGAR, JANET, spouse of John McBurnie a cordiner in Dumfries, testament, 1686, Comm. Dumfries. [NRS]

EDGAR, JOHN, was admitted as a burgess of Dumfries in 1665, [DBR]; Deacon of the Squaremen of Dumfries, testament, 1684. [NRS]

EDGAR, JOHN, from Dumfries, a member of the Scots Charitable Society of Boston in 1694. [NEHGS/SCS]

EDGAR, JOHN, a barber in Dumfries, testament, 1742, Comm. Dumfries, [NRS]

EDGAR, ROBERT, a weaver, was admitted as a burgess of Dumfries, 1777. [DBR]

EDGAR, ROBERT, a chapman, was admitted as a burgess of Dumfries, 1791. [DBR]

EDGAR, THOMAS, of Reidbank, born 1661, Provost of Dumfries, died 14 September 1739, husband of Janet Reid. [St Michael's MI]; a deed, 1715. [NRS.RD4.116.140]; testaments, 1744, 1747, Comm. Dumfries. [NRS]

EDGAR, WILLIAM, was admitted as a burgess of Dumfries in 1665, [DBR]; a writer in Dumfries, subscribed to the Test, 1683. [RPCS.VIII.640]

EDMISTON, JAMES, a merchant in Dumfries, 1621. [NRS.E71.10.5]

EGGAR, JOHN, a wigmaker in Dumfries, 1707. [NRS.AC9.246]

ERSKINE, JAMES, Lord Grange, was admitted a burgess of Dumfries, 1709. [NRS.GD124.18.59]

ERSKINE, ROBERT, a merchant, was admitted as a burgess of Dumfries, 1751. [DBR]

ESKDALE, HERRIES, in Dumfries, testament, 1796, Comm. Dumfries. [NRS]

ESKDALE, ROBERT, a merchant in Dumfries, testament, 1740, Comm. Dumfries. [NRS]

EWART, ARCHIBALD, a wright, was admitted as a burgess of Dumfries, 1756. [DBR]; testament, 1795, Comm. Dumfries. [NRS]

EWART, DOUGAL, a merchant, was admitted as a burgess of Dumfries, 1750. [DBR]

EWART, JOHN, a merchant, was admitted as a burgess of Dumfries, 1752. [DBR]; a merchant bailie of Dumfries, testaments, 1767, Comm. Dumfries. [NRS]

EUART, JOHN, the younger, a merchant, was admitted as a burgess of Dumfries in 1790, [DBR]; a bailie of Dumfries, 1707. [EUL.LC3606]

EWART, JOHN, a merchant in Dumfries, a deed, 1715. [NRS.RD2.105.304]

EWART, JOHN, a vintner, was admitted as a burgess of Dumfries, 1737. [DBR]

EWART, JOHN, Provost of Dumfries, 1741. [NRS.AC9.1471]

EWART, MARGARET, relict of Andrew Bell a merchant in Dumfries, testament, 1717, Comm. Dumfries. [NRS]

EWART, THOMAS, in Dumfries, testament, 1782, Comm. Dumfries, [NRS]

EWART, WILLIAM, was admitted as a burgess of Dumfries in 1713, [DBR]; merchant in Dumfries, a deed, 1715. [NRS.RD2.105.304]

EWING, JOHN, a shoemaker, was admitted as a burgess of Dumfries, 1768. [DBR]

EWING, WILLIAM, a shoemaker, was admitted as a burgess of Dumfries, 1741. [DBR]; testament, 1789, Comm. Dumfries. [NRS]

FAIRIES, JAMES, was admitted as a burgess of Dumfries in 1668, [DBR]; a tailor burgess of Dumfries, testament, 1674, Comm. Dumfries. [NRS]

FAIRIES, JAMES, a merchant, was admitted as a burgess of Dumfries in 1738. [DBR]

FARRIS, JOHN, was admitted as a burgess of Dumfries in 1728, [DBR]; a merchant in Dumfries, an adjudication, 1741. [NRS.CS228.A2.28]

FAIRIES, JOHN, a merchant, was admitted as a burgess of Dumfries in 1744. [DBR]

FAREIS, WILLIAM, a merchant burgess of Dumfries, testament, 1609, Comm. Edinburgh. [NRS]

FALCONER, MARY, widow of George Gilchrist, residing in Dumfries, testament, 1776, Comm. Dumfries. [NRS]

FERGUSON, ALEXANDER, at the Bridgend of Dumfries, testament, 1687, Comm. Dumfries. [NRS]

FERGUSON, ALEXANDER, of Craigdarroch, was admitted a burgess of Dumfries in 1708. [NRS.GD77.196.2]

FERGUSON, ALEXANDER, master of the Success of Dumfries, 1741. [NRS.AC9.1471]; master of the Adventure of Dumfries trading with Virginia, 1748. [NRS.CS16.1.80]

FERGUSON, ELIZABETH, wife of Cuthbert Amullgain a merchant burgess of Dumfries, testament, 1629, Comm. Dumfries. [NRS]

FERGUSON, GEORGE, an advocate, was admitted as a burgess of Dumfries in 1792. [DBR]

FERGUSON, HENRIETTA, daughter of the late Alexander Ferguson an advocate, residing in Dumfries, testament.1799, Comm. Dumfries. [NRS]

FERGUSON JAMES, a Roman Catholic in Rigside, Dumfries, 1704. [NAS.CH1.5.2]

FERGUSON, JANET, in Dumfries, testament, 1789, Comm. Dumfries. [NRS]

FERGUSON, JOHN, a tobacconist, was admitted as a burgess of Dumfries in 1742. [DBR]

FERGUSON, JOHN, a surgeon, was admitted as a burgess of Dumfries in 1750. [DBR]

FERGUSON, JOHN, a glazier, was admitted as a burgess of Dumfries in 1776. [DBR]

FERGUSON, MARGARET, in Dumfries, testament, 1738, Comm. Dumfries. [NRS]

FERGUSON, ROBERT, a merchant burgess of Dumfries, testament, 1638, Comm. Dumfries. [NRS]

FERGUSON, ROBERT, was admitted as a burgess of Dumfries in 1688, [DBR]; a dyer in Dumfries, 1707. [EUL.LC.3036]

FERGUSON, ROBERT, a merchant in Dumfries, 1741, [NRS.AC9.1471]; 1755-1760. [NRS.GD77.2044]

FERGUSON, ROBERT, an innkeeper, was admitted as a burgess of Dumfries in 1770. [DBR]

FERGUSON, ROBERT, a meal-dealer, was admitted as a burgess of Dumfries in 1785. [DBR]

FERGUSON, WILLIAM, a merchant, was admitted as a burgess of Dumfries in 1740. [DBR]; testament, 1770, Comm. Dumfries. [NRS]

FERGUSON, WILLIAM, a merchant, was admitted as a burgess of Dumfries in 1761. [DBR]

FINDLATOR, PETER, a saddler, was admitted as a burgess of Dumfries in 1798. [DBR]

FINDLAY, ANDREW, a merchant in Dumfries, testament, 1794, Comm. Dumfries, [NRS]

FINDLAY, CHARLES, a gardener, was admitted as a burgess of Dumfries in 1768. [DBR]

FINGLASS, WILLIAM, was admitted as a burgess of Dumfries in 1668, [DBR]; a bailie of Dumfries, testament, 1687. Comm. Dumfries. [NRS]

FINLAW, JAMES, a tailor, was admitted as a burgess of Dumfries in 1749. [DBR]

FINLAY, ..., a tobacconist in Dumfries, 1786. [NRS.CE51.Letterbook]

FINNIS, WILLIAM, was admitted as a burgess of Dumfries in 1668, [DBR]; a bailie of Dumfries, accused of allowing a prisoner to escape from Dumfries Tolbooth in 1683. [RPCS.VIII.152]

FISHER, EDWARD, arrived in Dumfries from Ireland in 1690. [NAS.CH2.537.15.1/29]

FISHER, THOMAS, a sailor, was admitted as a burgess of Dumfries in 1739. [DBR]

FLEMING, JOHN, a burgess of Dumfries, accused of liberating a prisoner from Dumfries Prison, 1600. [RPCS.VI.636]

FLEMING, MARGARET, daughter of Leonard Fleming late Excise Supervisor in Dumfries, testament, 1798, Comm. Dumfries. [NRS]

FORBES, DAVID, in Dumfries, formerly a merchant in Ramsay, Isle of Man, testament, 1771, Comm. Dumfries. [NRS]

FORSYTH, JOHN, servant of John Kennan, a wright in Dumfries, aged about 20 and unmarried, a witness, 1687. [RPCS.XIII.169]

FORSYTH, MATTHEW, residing in Dumfries, suspected of Catholicism, 1601. [RPCS.VI.312]; a merchant burgess of Dumfries, husband of Janet Neilson, testament, 1605, Comm. Edinburgh. [NRS]

FORSYTH, PETER, a merchant in Dumfries, 1621. [NRS.E71.10.5]

FORSYTH, ROBERT, a tailor burgess of Dumfries, 1601. [RPCS.VI.263]

FRASER, ALEXANDER, a staymaker, was admitted as a burgess of Dumfries in 1783. [DBR]

FRASER, ANDREW, a flax-dresser, was admitted as a burgess of Dumfries in 1773. [DBR]

FRASER, ANDREW, an innkeeper in Dumfries, testament, 1800, Comm. Dumfries. [NRS]

FRASER, DAVID, a merchant burgess of Dumfries, testament, 1642, Comm. Dumfries. [NRS]

FRASER, HUGH, of Laggan, Commissary Clerk of Dumfries, testaments, 1744, 1755, Comm. Dumfries. [NRS]

FRASER, JOHN, was admitted as a burgess of Dumfries in 1672, [DBR]; schoolmaster in Dumfries, a deed, 1684. [NRS.RD4.53.816]

FRASER, JOHN, a merchant, was admitted as a burgess of Dumfries in 1764. [DBR]; testament, 1796, Comm. Dumfries. [NRS]

FRASER, THOMAS, a thread maker in Dumfries, testament, 1778, Comm. Dumfries. [NRS]

FRASER, THOMAS, a merchant, was admitted as a burgess of Dumfries in 1798. [DBR]

FREW, EBENEZER, a merchant, was admitted as a burgess of Dumfries in 1768. [DBR]

FROOD, JOHN, a tailor, was admitted as a burgess of Dumfries in 1775. [DBR]

FRUID, JANET, spouse of John Paterson a cordiner burgess of Dumfries, a testament, 1627, Comm. Dumfries. [NRS]

FULLARTON, HUGH, a barber, was admitted as a burgess of Dumfries in 1750. [DBR]

FUNNANE, KATHERINE, relict of William McKinnell late Deacon of the Smiths, and Convenor of the Trades of Dumfries, testaments, 1680, 1681, Comm. Dumfries. [NRS]

FURMONT, ROBERT, a maltman burgess of Dumfries, testament, 1638, Comm. Dumfries. [NRS]

GARDINER, WILLIAM, a gardener, was admitted as a burgess of Dumfries in 1755. [DBR]; testament, 1780, Comm. Dumfries. [NRS]

GARMORIE, ROBERT, a wright, was admitted as a burgess of Dumfries in 1750. [DBR]

GASS, JOHN, a barber, was admitted as a burgess of Dumfries in 1750. [DBR]

GASS, JOSEPH, was admitted as a burgess of Dumfries in 1790, [DBR]; a tobacconist in Dumfries, 1786. [NRS.CE51.Letterbook]

GAY, WILLIAM, in Dumfries, a sasine, 1779. [NRS.RS23.XXII. 209]; a horse hirer in Dumfries, testament, 1781, Comm. Dumfries. [NRS]

GEDDES, JOHN, a bailie burgess of Dumfries, a bond, 1632. [NRS.GD34.466]

GEDDES, MUNGO, a merchant burgess of Dumfries, testament, 1631, Comm. Dumfries. [NRS]

GEDDIS, THOMAS, a Customs officer at Dumfries, 1784. [NRS.CE51.2/3]

GEIR, GEORGE, a burgess of Dumfries, husband of Jane Bell, testament, 1600, Comm. Edinburgh. [NRS]

GIBSON, ANDREW, a weaver, was admitted as a burgess of Dumfries in 1765. [DBR]

GIBSON, EBENEZER, a shopkeeper, was admitted as a burgess of Dumfries in 1765. [DBR]; testament, 1770, Comm. Dumfries. [NRS]

GIBSON, JAMES, a flesher, was admitted as a burgess of Dumfries in 1737. [DBR]; Deacon of the Fleshers of Dumfries, testaments, 1757, 1777, Comm. Dumfries. [NRS]

GIBSON, JAMES, jr., a flesher, was admitted as a burgess of Dumfries in 1764. [DBR]

GIBSON, JAMES, a flesher, was admitted as a burgess of Dumfries in 1764. [DBR]

GIBSON, JAMES, a merchant from Dumfries, settled in Suffolk, Virginia, by 1769, dead by 1788. [NRS.RD4.204.2; CS17.1.7/11; RS23.XX.372]

GIBSON, JANET, spouse of George Thomson a merchant burgess of Dumfries, testament, 1630, Comm. Dumfries. [NRS]

GIBSON, JOHN, residing in Dumfries, suspected of Catholicism, 1601. [RPCS.VI.312]

GIBSON, JOHN, a notary in Dumfries, 1687. [RPCS.XIII.156]

GIBSON, JOHN, a merchant in Dumfries, testament [missing] 1703, Comm. Dumfries. [NRS]

GIBSON, JOHN, a tailor, was admitted as a burgess of Dumfries in 1740. [DBR]

GIBSON, JOHN, a flesher, was admitted as a burgess of Dumfries in 1797. [DBR]

GIBSON, JOSEPH, a vintner, was admitted as a burgess of Dumfries in 1798.
[DBR]

GIBSON, ROBERT, a notary burgess of Dumfries, testament, 1643, Comm.
Dumfries. [NRS]

GIBSON, ROBERT, a merchant in Dumfries, testament, 1730, Comm.
Dumfreis. [NRS]

GIBSON, THOMAS, master of the Fleshers of Dumfries, 1661.
[DAC]

GIBSON, THOMAS, a flesher, was admitted as a burgess of Dumfries in 1754.
[DBR]

GIBSON, THOMAS, Deacon of the Trades of Dumfries, 1762.
[NRS.CS27.1.43300]

GIBSON, WILLIAM, a flesher, was admitted as a burgess of Dumfries in 1772.
[DBR]

GILCHRIST, EBENEZER, MD, a physician in Dumfries, husband
of Grisel Corrie, sasines, 1763/1767. [NRS.RS23.XIX.194; XX.82]
; born 1707, died 1774. [St Michael's MI]

GILCHRIST, JAMES, a bailie of Dumfries, 1733. [NRS.AC11.71]

GILCHRIST, JOHN, a bailie of Dumfries, accused of allowing a prisoner to
escape from Dumfries Tolbooth in 1683. [RPCS.VIII.152]; testament [missing]
1705, Comm. Dumfries. [NRS]

GILCHRIST, JOHN, a merchant bailie of Dumfries, testament,
1734, Comm. Dumfries. [NRS]

GILCHRIST, Dr JOHN, born 1747, a physician in Dumfries, died
10 September 1830, husband of Grizzel Corrie, parents of John,
Marion, Grizzel, Janet, and Anne. [St Michael's MI, Dumfries]

GILCHRIST, THOMAS, a merchant in Dumfries, 1622.
[NRS.E71.10.5]

GILCHRIST, THOMAS, a merchant in Dumfries, 1735.
[NRS.GD18.5395]; 1733, [NRS.AC11.71]; testaments, 1748, 1750,
Comm. Dumfries. [NRS]

GILCHRIST, THOMAS, son of Thomas Gilchrist in Dumfries, settled in Suffolk, Virginia, and in Halifax, North Carolina, before 1769. [NRS.RD4.235.686][VaGaz.952/1014]

GILCHRIST, WILLIAM, in Dumfries, 1727. [NRS.AC9.1015]

GILHAGIE, JOHN, a merchant in Dumfries, testament, 1725, Comm. Dumfries. [NRS]

GILLESPIE, JOHN, a merchant, was admitted as a burgess of Dumfries in 1735. [DBR]; testament, 1768, Comm. Dumfries. [NRS]

GILLESPIE, JOHN, a flesher, was admitted as a burgess of Dumfries in 1798. [DBR]

GILLISON, AMBROSE, a merchant, was admitted as a burgess of Dumfries in 1737. [DBR]

GILLISON, WILLIAM, died 24 May 1700. [St Michael's MI, Dumfries]

GLAISTERS, JOSEPH, a tanner, was admitted as a burgess of Dumfries in 1757. [DBR]

GLASSELL, JOHN, son of Robert Glassell a blacksmith burgess of Dumfries, deceased by 1630. [NRS.GD1.202.32]

GLASSELL, JOHN, born 1734, a merchant from Dumfries, settled in Oxford, Maryland, 1762, in Fredericksburg, Spotsylvania, 1772, later in Longniddry, Scotland, 1779, died 1806. [NRS.RGS. 119.271; RS27.247.237] [VaGaz.822/1108/1184] [MdGaz.921]

GLEDSTANES, THOMAS, in Dumfries, 1693. [EUL.LC2908]

GLEN, DANIEL, a writer, was admitted as a burgess of Dumfries in 1767. [DBR]

GLEN, DAVID, an innkeeper in Dumfries, testament, 1767, Comm. Dumfries. [NRS]

GLEN, WILLIAM, a litster in Dumfries, sasines, 1778. [NRS.RS23.XXII.119/180]

GLENCORSE, JANET, spouse of John Burgess sr., a weaver in Dumfries, 1687. [RPCS.XIII.170]

GLENCORSE, JEAN, a widow in Dumfries, mother of Elizabeth McNaught, a court case, 1688. [RPCS.XIII.204]

GLENCORSE, THOMAS, a merchant in Dumfries, 1621, [NRS.E71.10.5]; testament, 1626, Comm. Dumfries. [NRS]

GLENDINNING, JAMES, in Kirkgait, Dumfries, a burgess of Dumfries, testament, 1625, Comm. Dumfries. [NRS]

GLENDINNING, JAMES, a chapman in Dumfries, son of Mathew Glendinning a workman in Dumfries, testament, 1638, Comm.Dumfries. [NRS]

GLENDINNING, JOHN, a currier, was admitted as a burgess of Dumfries in 1739. [DBR]

GLENDENNING, WILLIAM, a merchant in Dumfries, 1621. [NRS.E71.10.5]

GLENDINNING, WILLIAM, a cooper, was admitted as a burgess of Dumfries in 1764. [DBR]

GLOVER, JAMES, a plasterer, was admitted as a burgess of Dumfries in 1798. [DBR]

GLOVER, JOSEPH, a tobacconist in Dumfries, 1786. [NRS.CE51.Letterbook]

GOLDIE, ALEXANDER, a Writer to the Signet, was admitted as a burgess of Dumfries in 1761. [DBR]

GOLDIE, JAMES, a flesher burgess of Dumfries, testament, 1685, Comm.Dumfries. [NRS]

GOLDIE, JAMES, emigrated from Dumfries aboard the Nannie and Jenny, master William Maxwell, bound for Virginia, 1749. [NRS.CS96.216/9]

GOLDIE, JAMES, a bricklayer, was admitted as a burgess of Dumfries in 1757. [DBR]

GOLDIE, JOHN, of Craigmuie, Commissary of Dumfries, was admitted as a burgess of Dumfries in 1735. [DBR]; 1735. [NRS.AC13.2.27]

GOLDIE, ROBERT, a merchant, was admitted as a burgess of Dumfries in 1737. [DBR]

GOLDIE, ROBERT, a flesher, was admitted as a burgess of Dumfries in 1762. [DBR]

GOLDIE, THOMAS, a merchant burgess of Dumfries, testament, 1638, Comm. Dumfries. [NRS]

GOLDIE, THOMAS, a merchant burgess of Dumfries, testament, 1686, Comm. Dumfries. [NRS]

GOLDIE, THOMAS, a tailor in Dumfries, 1707. [NRS.AC9.246]

GOOD, ROBERT, at the Bridgend of Dumfries, testament, 1687, Comm. Dumfries. [NRS]

GORDON, ALEXANDER, a surgeon, was admitted as a burgess of Dumfries in 1747. [DBR]

GORDON, ALEXANDER, a gardener, was admitted as a burgess of Dumfries in 1754. [DBR]

GORDON, ALEXANDER, of Crogo, residing in Dumfries, testament, 1780, Comm. Dumfries. [NRS]

GORDON, ANNA, daughter of George Gordon of Troquhain, residing in Dumfries, testament, 1782, Comm. Dumfries. [NRS]

GORDON, ARCHIBALD, a collector, was admitted as a burgess of Dumfries in 1745. [DBR]; testament, 1756, Comm. Dumfries. [NRS]

GORDON, GEORGE, a merchant, was admitted as a burgess of Dumfries in 1737. [DBR]

GORDON, GEORGE, of Troquhen, residing in Dumfries, testaments, 1759, 1761, 1770, Comm. Dumfries. [NRS]

GORDON, GEORGE, son of the late George Gordon of Troquhen, residing in Dumfries, testament, 1782, Comm. Dumfries. [NRS]

GORDON, GILBERT, a merchant, was admitted as a burgess of Dumfries in 1746. [DBR]

GORDON, GILBERT, Excise collector in Dumfries, 1762. [NRS.CS271.43300]; received a bill of exchange from Robert Palmer in Bath, North Carolina, to pay to Gabriel Cathcart, in 1766. [NRS.GD180.352]

GORDON, JAMES, a merchant in Dumfries, a deed, 1697. [NRS.RD4.80.143]

GORDON, JAMES, a writer in Dumfries, 1708. [NRS.AC8.101]

GORDON, JOHN, a dyer at the Bridgend of Dumfries, testament, 1737, Comm. Dumfries. [NRS]

GORDON, JOHN, a tailor in Dumfries, was admitted as a burgess of Dumfries in 1757, [DBR]; imprisoned for rioting in 1759, sentenced to transportation to the colonies 15 December 1760. [NRS.JC27]

GORDON, JOHN, a tailor, was admitted as a burgess of Dumfries in 1769. [DBR]

GORDON, JOHN and ROBERT, writers in Dumfries, versus Charles Thomson in North America, 6 July 1778. [NRS.CS16.1.174]

GORDON, MARGARET, in Dumfries, relict of Nathaniel Duke, testament, 1763, Comm. Dumfries. [NRS]

GORDON, MARY, in Dumfries, daughter of the late Robert Gordon of Auchendolly, testament, 1798, Comm. Dumfries. [NRS]

GORDON, Brigadier General PATRICK, of King's Grange, residing in Dumfries, testament, 1780, Comm. Dumfries. [NRS]

GORDON, ROBERT, a tailor, was admitted as a burgess of Dumfries in 1764. [DBR]

GORDON, ROBERT, a writer in Dumfries, testaments, 1790, 1796.Comm. Dumfries. [NRS]

GORDON, SAMUEL, a merchant burgess of Dumfries, 1682. [NAS.GD78.160]; a letter, 1708. [NRS.RH15.120.148]; TESTAMENT [MISSING] 1713, Comm. Dumfries. [NRS]

GORDON, THOMAS, a surgeon in Dumfries, testament, 1767, Comm. Dumfries. [NRS]

GORDON, THOMAS, born 1766, a wine merchant, died 12 January 1813, husband of Agnes Kirkpatrick, parents of Sarah and William who drowned near Canton aged 17. [St Michael's MI, Dumfries]

GORDON, WILLIAM, a writer in Dumfries, a witness in 1687. [RPCS.XIII. 156]

GOURLAY, THOMAS, a burgess of Dumfries, testament, 1629, Comm. Dumfries. [NRS]

GRACIE, JAMES, son of James Gracie and his wife Jean Cowan, Brevet Major of the 21st Infantry, died 13 September 1813 at the Battle of Baltimore. [St Michael's MI, Dumfries]

GRAHAM, ARCHIBALD, master of the Neptune of Dumfries arrived in Charleston, South Carolina, in December 1735. [TNA.CO5.509]

GRAHAM, ARTHUR, in Dumfries, a summons, 1695. [NAS.GD137.494]

GRAHAM, GEORGE, a merchant in Dumfries, 1621. [NRS.E71.10.5]

GRAHAM, JAMES, a ship-owner in Dumfries, 1727. [NRS.AC9.1020]

GRAHAM, JOHN, a merchant, was admitted as a burgess of Dumfries in 1741. [DBR]

GRAHAM, Captain JOHN, master of the Jean of Dumfries, was admitted a burgess of Dumfries, 1750. [NRS.GD1.402.70]

GRAHAM, JOHN, jr., a merchant in Dumfries, and James McIntosh, late merchant in Jamaica, versus Arbuthnott and Guthrie merchants in Edinburgh, 1780. [NRS.CS16.1.179]

GRAHAM, JOSEPH, a shoemaker, was admitted as a burgess of Dumfries in 1767. [DBR]

GRAHAM, MARY, relict of James Stewart a merchant in Dumfries, testament, 1749, Comm. Dumfries, [NRS]

GRAHAM, RICHARD, a merchant from Dumfries, settled in Prince William County, Virginia, by 1757. [VMHB.19.94][NRS.CS17.1.1/97][VaGaz. 668/1243]

GRAHAM, ROBERT, bailie and merchant burgess of Dumfries, and his wife Jean Douglas, were granted land in the parsh of Kirkpatrick, 1653. [RGS.X.111]

GRAHAM, ROBERT, late Provost of Dumfries, a tack, 1665. [NAS.GD77.175/3]

GRAHAM, ROBERT, a merchant in Dumfries, father of William Graham, 1679. [NAS.AC7/5]

GRAHAM, ROBERT, a smith in Dumfries, testament, 1740, Comm. Dumfries. [NRS]

GRAHAM, ROBERT, a flesher, was admitted as a burgess of Dumfries in 1744. [DBR]

GRAHAM, WILLIAM, a merchant in Dumfries, 1679. [NRS.AC7.5]

GRAHAM, WILLIAM, in Dumfries, testament, 1775, Comm. Dumfries. [NRS]

GRANGER, WILLIAM, a tobacconist in Dumfries, 1786. [NRS.CE51.Letterbook]

GRANT, JAMES, a merchant, was admitted as a burgess of Dumfries in 1798. [DBR]

GRIER, AGNES, spouse of John Panie at the Bridgend of Dumfries, testament, 1680, Comm. Dumfries. [NRS]

GRIER, JAMES, son of William Grier late Deacon of the Weavers in Dumfries, 1705. [NRS.GD1.1261.1]

GREIR, WILLIAM, a merchant in Dumfries, 1622. [NRS.E71.10.5]

GRIERSON, ELIZABETH, spouse of Thomas Forsyth late Deacon of the Fleshers, testament, 1662, Comm. Dumfries. [NRS]

GRIERSON, JAMES, an under-teacher in Dumfries, later schoolmaster at Ormiston by 1680, husband of Janet Douglas, a deed, 1668. [NRS.RD4.22.356]

GRIERSON, JAMES, a tailor, was admitted as a burgess of Dumfries in 1750. [DBR]

GRIERSON, JOHN, a messenger in Dumfries, testament, 1681, Comm. Dumfries. [NRS]

GRIERSON, JOHN, a dyer, was admitted as a burgess of Dumfries in 1737 [DBR]; a dyer in Dumfries, a sasine, 1768. [NRS.GD77.164]; testament, 1797, Comm. Dumfries. [NRS]

GRIERSON, JOHN, a bookseller, was admitted as a burgess of Dumfries in 1739. [DBR]

GRIERSON, JOSEPH, a meal dealer, was admitted as a burgess of Dumfries in 1799. [DBR]

GRIERSON, MARION, spouse of William Burnet a merchant in Dumfries, a sasine, 17 April 1725. [NRS.RS23.10.181]

GRIERSON, ROBERT, a merchant in Dumfries, testament, 1755, Comm. Dumfries. [NRS]

GRIERSON, THOMAS, a dyer, was admitted as a burgess of Dumfries in 1759. [DBR]

GRIERSON, WILLIAM, a writer in Dumfries, a witness, 1688. [ROCS.XIII. 284]

GRIERSON, WILLIAM, a shopkeeper, was admitted as a burgess of Dumfries in 1762. [DBR]

GRIEVE, GEORGE, a merchant in Dumfries, testaments, 1799, 1800, Comm. Dumfries. [NRS]

GRIEVE, JAMES, a merchant in Dumfries, 1798. [NRS.CS97.112.96]

GRIVE, THOMAS, in Dumfries, a family bible with notes of births and deaths of family members, 1758-1798 including those in Newfoundland. [NRS.CS96.231]

GUNOCHAN, ADAM, a shoemaker in Dumfries, testament [missing]1702, Comm. Dumfries. [NRS]

GUNYEON, WILLIAM, a tobacconist, was admitted as a burgess of Dumfries in 1765. [DBR]

GUTHRIE, GEORGE, a merchant, was admitted as a burgess of Dumfries in 1744. [DBR]

HAINING, ALEXANDER, in Dumfries, 1684. [RPCS.XIII.169]

HAINING, DAVID, a dyer, was admitted as a burgess of Dumfries in 1754. [DBR]

HAINING, JOHN, a bricklayer, was admitted as a burgess of Dumfries in 1765. [DBR]

HAIR, GEORGE, born 1789, son of Ninian Hair, died 27 February 1812 in St Thomas, Jamaica. [Dumfries MI]

HAIR, NORMAN, a dyer, was admitted as a burgess of Dumfries in 1768. [DBR]

HAIRSTANES, JOHN, a merchant burgess of Dumfries, 1621, [NRS.E71.10.5]; heir to his brother Michael Hairstanes of Craigs, 1629. [NRS.Retours.Dumfries.139]

HAIRSTANES, JOHN, a shoemaker, was admitted as a burgess of Dumfries in 1765. [DBR]

HALLIDAY, GEORGE, a Customs officer at Dumfries, 1784. [NRS.CE51.2/3]

HALLIDAY, MARTHA, and her spouse William Dalziel a merchant in Dumfries, decree, 1772. [NRS.CS229.M3.16]

HALLIDAY, SIMON, a merchant in Dumfries, testament, 1684, Comm. Dumfries. [NRS]

HALIDAY, THOMAS, a merchant in Dumfries, 1621. [NRS.E71.10.5]

HAMILTON, EDWARD, Customs Controller in Dumfries, 1613-1621. [NRS.E74.1/4; E74.2/4.7; E71.10.5/7]

HAMILTON, WILLIAM, Customs riding officer at Dumfries, testament, 1772, Comm. Dumfries. [NRS]

HAMILTON, WILLIAM, a merchant in Dumfries, testament, 1800, Comm. Dumfries. [NRS]

HANNA, JOHN, a gardener, was admitted as a burgess of Dumfries in 1746. [DBR]

HANNAH, CHARLES, an innkeeper, was admitted as a burgess of Dumfries in 1771. [DBR]

HANNAH, JOHN, born 1761, a merchant in the West Indies, died 20 July 1841, [St Michael's MI, Dumfries]

HANNAH, ROBERT, a shoemaker, was admitted as a burgess of Dumfries in 1762. [DBR]

HANNA, WILLIAM, a Covenanter imprisoned in Dumfries Tolbooth, transported to East New Jersey in 1685. [RPCS.XI.94/154]

HANNAY, AGNES, in Dumfries, daughter of Robert Hannay late Deacon of the Shoemakers in Dumfries, testament, 1800, Comm. Dumfries. [NRS]

HARKNESS, ROBERT, cooper at the Bridgend of Dumfries, husband of Agnes Farquhar, a sasine, 1773. [NRS.RS23.XXI.56]

HARKNESS, WILLIAM, a farmer, [1776-1848], husband of Elizabeth Corrie, parents of Walter Harkness, [1801-1834], a surgeon in Canada. [Dumfries MI]

HARLEY, JAMES, a joiner, was admitted as a burgess of Dumfries in 1737. [DBR]

HARLEY, JOHN, a surgeon in Dumfries, sasines, 1773-1778. [NRS.RS23.XXI. 88; XXII.113]

HARPER, ALEXANDER, a wright in Dumfries, testament, 1740, Comm. Dumfries. [NRS]

HAUGH, ISOBEL, widow of Thomas Kerr a merchant in Dumfries, testament, 1776, Comm. Dumfries. [NRS]

HAWTHORN, WILLIAM, a weaver, was admitted as a burgess of Dumfries in 1746. [DBR]

HAY, EBENEZER, a wigmaker, was admitted as a burgess of Dumfries in 1750. [DBR]

HAYNING, WILLIAM, a merchant in Dumfries, 1621. [NRS.E71.10.5]

HENDERSON, HUGH, alias HEW HENDRYSON, educated at Edinburgh University, graduated MA in 1632, minister of St Michael's, Dumfries, 1648-1662.[F.2.26]

HENDERSON, JAMES, a merchant in Dumfries, testament, 1745, Comm. Dumfries. [NRS]

HENDERSON, JANET, relict of Thomas Henderson a smith in Dumfries, testament, 1763, Comm. Dumfries. [NRS]

HENDERSON, JOHN, a shopkeeper, was admitted as a burgess of Dumfries in 1767. [DBR]

HENDERSON, PATRICK, a shoemaker, was admitted as a burgess of Dumfries in 1748. [DBR]; testament, 1770, Comm. Dumfries. [NRS]

HENDERSON, THOMAS, a smith, was admitted as a burgess of Dumfries in 1736. [DBR]

HENDERSON, WILLIAM, a smith, was admitted as a burgess of Dumfries in 1753. [DBR]

HENDRY, HELEN, spouse of Hew Conteine a merchant burgess of Dumfries, testament, 1629, Comm. Dumfries. [NRS]

HEPBURN, EBENEZER, a merchant, was admitted as a burgess of Dumfries in 1739. [DBR]

HEPBURN, EBENEZER, a Customs officer at Dumfries, 1784. [NRS.CE51.2/3]

HEPBURN, JOHN, an innkeeper, was admitted as a burgess of Dumfries in 1745. [DBR]

HEPBURN, ROBERT, a chapman, was admitted as a burgess of Dumfries in 1742. [DBR]

HEPBURN, WILLIAM, a tutor from Dumfries, emigrated to Virginia 1774. [NLS.McMurdo-Maxwell pp]

HERRIES, CATHERINE, widow of the late John Rome a bailie of Dumfries, 1707. [EUL.LC3036]

HERRIES, JAMES, a merchant in Dumfries, testament, 1681, Comm. Dumfries, [NRS]

HERRIES, JOHN, of Braco, residing in Dumfries, suspected of Catholicism, 1601. [RPCS.VI.312]

HERRIES, JOHN, a merchant in Dumfries, testament, 1722, Comm. Dumfries. [NRS]

HERRIES, KATHERINE, widow of bailie Rome, a Roman Catholic in Dumfries, 1704. [NRS.CH1.5.2]; testament, 1719, Comm. Dumfries. [NRS]

HERRIES, JAMES, a merchant in Dumfries, testament, 1681, Comm. Dumfries. [NRS]

HERRIES, JOHN, jr., a merchant in Dumfries, testament [missing] 1700, Comm. Dumfries. [NRS]

HERRIES, ROBERT, in Kililour, residing in Dumfries, suspected of Catholicism, 1601. [RPCS.VI.312]

HERRIES, JOHN, of Buss, town clerk of Dumfries, deeds, 1715. [NRS.RD2.104.958; RD2.104.457/466]

HERRIOT, ALEXANDER, a shoemaker, was admitted as a burgess of Dumfries in 1798. [DBR]

HERRIOT, JAMES, a dyer at the Bridgend of Dumfries, sasines, 1766-1767. [NRS.RS23.XIX.369/375/387; XX.142]

HERRIOT, WILLIAM, in Dumfries, a witness, 1687-1688. [RPCS.XIII.156/284]

HERRON, JAMES, a tailor, was admitted as a burgess of Dumfries in 1750. [DBR]

HILL, ELIZABETH, a spinning mistress in Dumfries, letters, 1748-1749. [NRS.GD18.5918]

HILL, GEORGE, a merchant in Dumfries, 1622. [NRS.E71.10.5]

HILL, GEORGE MCCARTNEY, born 1780, son of George Hill of Blaiket, [1743-1810], and his wife Jean Callendar, died 7 October 1813 in Tobago. [Dumfries MI]

HILL, JAMES, born 1775, son of George Hill of Blaiket, [1743-1810], and his wife Jean Callendar, a physician, died 12 June 1824 in St Croix, Danish West Indies. [Dumfries MI][BM. 16.488] [EA.4899.303]

HILL, JOHN, master of the Margaret of Dumfries in 1689, and of the Bonadventure of Dumfries in 1690. [NRS,E72.6.13/18]

HILLOCK, JAMES, a merchant in Dumfries, testaments, 1735, 1738, 1741, 1744, Comm. Dumfries. [NRS]

HODGE, JAMES, a merchant in Dumfries, testament, 1744. Comm. Dumfries. [NRS]

HOGG, ANDREW, Deacon of the Incorporation of Squaremen of Dumfries, testament, 1792, Comm. Dumfries. [NRS]

HOGG, ANDREW, an inn-keeper in Dumfries, 1786. [NRS.CE51.Letterbook]

HOGG, CHARLES, a weaver, was admitted as a burgess of Dumfries in 1761. [DBR]

HOGG, JOHN, son of James Hogg, a draper in Dumfries, [1768-1833], and his wife Annie Stewart, died in New York aged 33 years. [Dumfries MI]

HOLDING, ALEXANDER, a weaver in Dumfries, testament, 1751, Comm. Dumfries. [NRS]

HOOD, JOHN, a weaver in Dumfries, testament, 1734, Comm. Dumfries. [NRS]

HOOD, JOHN, a gardener, was admitted as a burgess of Dumfries in 1768. [DBR]

HOPE, JAMES, a shipmaster in Dumfries, 1727. [NRS.AC9.979]

HOPE, JAMES, a banker, was admitted as a burgess of Dumfries in 1797. [DBR]

HOPE, WILLIAM, a barber, was admitted as a burgess of Dumfries in 1766. [DBR]

HOPKINS, MARY, spouse of Robert McCair, a Roman Catholic in Dumfries, 1704. [NRS.CH1.5.2]

HORNER, EDWARD, residing in Dumfries, suspected of Catholicism, 1601. [RPCS.VI.312]

HORSBURGH, ROBERT, a merchant in Dumfries, 1621.
[NRS.E71.10.5]

HOSSACK, JOHN, of Glengaber and Buff Bay River, Jamaica,
born 1756, died 19 October 1815. [Dumfries MI]

HOUSOUN, THOMAS, a merchant in Dumfries, 1622.
[NRS.E71.10.5]

HOUSTOUN, ARCHIBALD, a merchant, was admitted as a burgess of
Dumfries in 1749. [DBR]

HOWAT, ALEXANDER, at the Bridgend of Dumfries, sasines,
1767. [NRS.RS23.XX.2/3; XXI.369]

HOWAT, CHARLES, a smith at the Bridgend, was admitted as a burgess
of Dumfries in 1767. [DBR]

HOWAT, JAMES, a wright, was admitted as a burgess of Dumfries in 1759.
[DBR]

HOWAT, JANET, spouse of Robert Dickson a millwright at the Bridgend of
Dumfries, testament, 1779, Comm. Dumfries. [NRS]

HOWAT, JOHN, a barber, was admitted as a burgess of Dumfries in 1750.
[DBR]

HOWAT, JOHN, a barber, was admitted as a burgess of Dumfries in 1770.
[DBR]

HOWAT, ROBERT, at the Bridgend of Dumfries, a deed. 1715.
[NRS.RD2.105.21]; testament, 1752, Comm. Dumfries. [NRS]

HOWAT, ROBERT, a tobacconist in Dumfries, 1786. [NRS.CE51.Letterbook]

HOWAT, WILLIAM, a shoemaker, was admitted as a burgess of Dumfries in
1743. [DBR]

HUDDLESTON, THOMAS, a cook, was admitted as a burgess of Dumfries in
1756. [DBR]

HUME, ANDREW, a waiter in Dumfries later in Edinburgh, a deed. 1715.
[NRS.RD4.116.243]

HUME, PATRICK, arrived in Dumfries from Ireland in 1690. [NRS.CH2.537.15.1/48]

HUNTER, ANDREW, minister of Greyfriars, Dumfries, from 1770 to 25 November 1772. [F.2.269]

HUNTER, DAVID, at the Bridgend of Dumfries, testament, 1659, Comm. Dumfries. [NRS]

HUNTER, DAVID, a merchant traveller, was admitted as a burgess of Dumfries in 1754. [DBR]

HUNTER, ELIZABETH, daughter of Andrew Hunter a merchant in Dumfries, testament, 1696, Comm. Dumfries. [NRS]

HUNTER, ROBERT, a shopkeeper, was admitted as a burgess of Dumfries in 1772. [DBR]

HUNTER, SAMUEL, born 1685 in Dumfries, an indentured servant, absconded from William Bradford in New York City in 1735. [N.Y.Gaz., 2.6.1735]

HUNTER, THOMAS, a surgeon-apothecary in Dumfries, testament, 1729, Comm. Dumfries. [NRS]

HUNTER, THOMAS, a merchant, was admitted as a burgess of Dumfries in 1751. [DBR]; testament, 1761, Comm. Dumfries. [NRS]

HUNTER, WILLIAM, a merchant, was admitted as a burgess of Dumfries in 1761. [DBR]

HUTCHISON, JOHN, a wheelwright at the Bridgend of Dumfries, a sasine, 1761. [NRS.RS23.XIX.3/249]

HUTTON, JOHN, a merchant, was admitted as a burgess of Dumfries in 1773. [DBR]

HUTTON, THOMAS, a dyer, was admitted as a burgess of Dumfries in 1735. [DBR]

HYND, JAMES, a merchant in Dumfries, a deed, 1697. [NRS.RD4.81.1102]

HYND, JOHN, of Drumcoltran, born 1738, died 1 June 1779. [St Michael's MI, Dumfries]

HYND, THOMAS, born February 1660, a merchant bailie of Dumfries, died 17 November 1739, husband of Agnes Edgar. [St Michael's MI, Dumfries]

HYSLOP, HELEN, spouse of John Nicolson a burgess of Dumfries, testament, 1630, Comm. Dumfries. [NRS]

HYSLOP, JAMES, a mason, was admitted as a burgess of Dumfries in 17959. [DBR]

HYSLOP, JOHN, a writer, was admitted as a burgess of Dumfries in 1761. [DBR]

HYSLOP, JOHN, a writer, was admitted as a burgess of Dumfries in 1764. [DBR]

HYSLOP, NICOL, a weaver burgess of Dumfries, testament, 1659, Comm. Dumfries. [NRS]

HYSLOP, WELLWOOD, born 1781, settled in Jamaica 1805, died 16 February 1845 in Kingston, Jamaica. [St Michael's MI, Dumfries]

HYSLOP, WILLIAM, a baker, was admitted as a burgess of Dumfries in 1767. [DBR]

INGLIS, MARY, arrived in Dumfries from Ireland in 1690. [NRS.CH2.537.15.1/40]

IRVINE, AGNES, daughter of the late John Irvine of Logan, versus Thomas Blackstock, her spouse, sometime in Dumfries, married there April 1751, a Process of Adherence, 1762. [NRS.CC8.6.388]

IRVINE, ALEXANDER, a writer in Dumfries, heir to his grand-father John Irvine of Drumcoltran, in 1713, also to his uncle John Irvine, son of John Irvine of Drumcoltran, in 1713, [NRS.S/H]; deed, 1714. [NRS.RD4.114.612]; testament, 1736, Comm. Dumfries. [NRS]

IRVINE, JOHN, bailie of Dumfries, a deed, 1691, husband of Rachel Wallace. [NRS.RD4.69.738]

IRVINE, JOHN, the elder, a merchant in Dumfries, a deed. 1715. [NRS.RD2.104.682]

IRVINE, JOHN, of Logan, Provost of Dumfries, deeds, 1714, 1715.
[NRS.RD2.103.1.708; TD2.103.2.404; RD4.114.673; RD2.105.127]

IRVINE, JOHN, of Logan, the younger, a merchant in Dumfries, tutor to
Christopher Irvine, deeds, 1714. [NRS.RD2.103.2.404; RD2.104.57]

IRVINE, JOHN, late Convenor of the Trades of Dumfries, 1727.
[NRS.AC8.353]

IRVING, AGNES, widow of John Brown a merchant in Dumfries, heir to her
brother Francis Irving in Dumfries, in 1714. [NRS.S/H]

IRVING, ANN, wife of Robert Anderson at the Bridgend of Dumfries, heir to
her grand-father Herbert Irving of Logan in 1740; and to her father James Irving
of Logan in 1740. [NRS.S/H]

IRVING, Mrs CATHERINE, in Dumfries, testament, 1799. Comm. Dumfries.
[NRS]

IRVING, FRANCIS, a merchant in Dumfries, trading with Flanders, 1622.
[NRS.E71.10.5]

IRVING, FRANCIS, Provost of Dumfries, testament, 1662, Comm. Dumfries.
[NRS]

IRVING, FRANCIS, a bailie in Dumfries, testament [missing] 1709, Comm.
Dumfries. [NRS]

IRVING, GEORGE, a merchant burgess of Dumfries, 1622. [NAS.E71.10.5];
testament, 1638, Comm. Dumfries. [NRS]

IRVING, HERBERT, a merchant burgess of Dumfries, husband of Isabel
Carlisle, testament, 1661, Comm. Dumfries. [NRS]

IRVING, JAMES, a bacon dealer at the Bridgend of Dumfries, records,
1794-1795. [NRS.CS96.752]

IRVING, JANET, heir to her father John Irving late Provost of Dumfries in
1713, also to her brother John Irving late bailie of Dumfries, 1713. [NRS.S/H]

IRVING, JOHN, a merchant in Dumfries, trading with Flanders, 1622.
[NRS.E71.10.5]

IRVING, JOHN, late Provost of Dumfries, land grant, 6 April 1666. [RGS.XI. 904]; merchant in Dumfries, papers 1659-1687. [NRS.GD472.47/88]; testaments, 1687, 1688, Comm. Dumfries. [NRS]

IRVING, JOHN, son of the deceased John Irving late Provost of Dumfries, was appointed a bailie of Dumfries in 1686 by King James VII. [RPCS.XIII.43]

IRVING, JOHN, of Drumcoltran, a bailie of Dumfries, 1693. [EUL.LC2908]

IRVING, JOHN, a merchant in Dumfries, a deed, 1699. [NRS.RD2.83.404]

IRVING, JOHN, the younger, a merchant in Dumfries, deeds, 1702. [NRS.RD2.86.1.438; RD2.86.2.567]

IRVING, JOHN, of Logan, see charter of 1707. [EUL.LC.3036]; Provost of Dumfries, deeds, 1702. [NRS.RD2.86.1.209/210/335/343]

IRVINE, JOHN, a bailie of Dumfries, a deed, 1702. [NRS.RD2.86.1.239]

IRVINE, JOHN, of Logan, Provost of Dumfries, heir to his father John Irvine of Logan in 1740. [NRS.S/H]

IRVING, JOHN, Convenor of the Trades of Dumfries, testaments, 1748, 1750, Comm. Dumfries. [NRS]

IRVING, JOHN, a shoemaker in Dumfries, a testament, 1758, Comm. Dumfries. [NRS]

IRVING, JOHN, a shoemaker, was admitted as a burgess of Dumfries in 1765. [DBR];

IRVING, JOHN, a shoemaker, was admitted as a burgess of Dumfries in 1790. [DBR]

IRVING, LUDOVICK, of Wisebie, a notorious thief, fled to Ireland, was captured there taken to Donaghadie then to Dumfries Tolbooth, from where he escaped in 1683. [RPCS.VIII.152]

IRVING, MARGARET, heir to her father John Irving late Provost of Dumfries in 1713, also to her brother John Irving of Drumcoltran, 1713. [NRS.S/H]

IRVING, MARIAN, heir to her father John Irving late Provost of Dumfries in 1713, also to her brother John Irving of Drumcoltran, 1713. [NRS.S/H]

IRVING, THOMAS, Provost of Dumfries, letters, 1666-1694.
[NRS.GD224.171.2]; a merchant in Dumfries, a deed, 1699.
[NRS.RD3.90.627]; testaments, 1675, 1682, Comm. Dumfries. [NRS]

IRVING, THOMAS, Receiver General of South Carolina, husband of Marion
Corbet, and Robert, Edward, and Marion Corbet, children of James Corbet,
merchant and late Provost of Dumfries, 6 August 1774. [NRS.CS16.1.161]

IRVING, WILLIAM, a prisoner in Dumfries, was murdered there by William
Douglas of Cashogle in 1602. [RPCS.VI.385]

IRVING, WILLIAM, a merchant in Dumfries, trading with Flanders, 1622.
[NRS.E71.10.5]; testament, 1639, Comm. Dumfries. [NRS]

IRVING, WILLIAM, jr., a merchant in Dumfries, testament, 1680, Comm.
Dumfries. [NRS]

IRVING, WILLIAM, a merchant in Dumfries, testament, 1743, Comm.
Dumfries. [NRS]

IRVING, WILLIAM, an Ensign of the 70th Regiment of Foot, a resident of
Dumfries, testament, 1799, Comm. Dumfries. [NRS]

IRVING, WINIFRED, daughter of William Irving a merchant in Dumfries, heir
to her grand-father convenor John Irving in Dumfries, in 1742. [NRS.S/H]

JACK, JOHN, a brewer in Dumfries, testament, 1714, Comm. Dumfries. [NRS]

JACKSON, ROBERT, a printer, was admitted as a burgess of Dumfries in 1787.
[DBR]

JAMIESON, THOMAS, a tobacconist in Dumfries, 1786.
[NRS.CE51.Letterbook]

JAIRDEN, WILLIAM, a merchant from Dumfries, a member of the Scots
Charitable Society of Boston in 1684. [NEHGS/SCSpp]

JARDINE, JAMES, a merchant in Dumfries, testament, 1729, Comm.
Dumfries. [NRS]

JARDINE, JAMES, a merchant, was admitted as a burgess of Dumfries in
1753. [DBR]

JARDINE, JOHN, a joiner, was admitted as a burgess of Dumfries in 1753 [DBR]

JARDINE, ROBERT, a writer in Dumfries, testament, 1746, Comm. Dumfries. [NRS]

JARDINE, ROBERT, a gardener, was admitted as a burgess of Dumfries in 1783. [DBR]

JARDINE, WILLIAM, in Dumfries, a surgeon in the Royal Navy, a testament, 1823. [NRS.CC5.21.58]

JARVIS, GEORGE, in Dumfries, a surgeon in the Royal Navy, testament, 1811. [NRS.CC10.2.7]

JOHNSTON, ADAM, a shoemaker, was admitted as a burgess of Dumfries in 1762. [DBR]

JOHNSTON, ANDREW, a merchant in Dumfries, 1621. [NRS.E71.10.5]

JOHNSTON, BESSIE, spouse of John Martin treasurer of Dumfries, testament, 1687, Comm. Dumfries. [NRS]

JOHNSTON, CATHERINE, relict of Edward Wilson a merchant in Dumfries, testament, 1709, Comm. Dumfries. [NRS]

JOHNSTON, CHARLES, a merchant in Ostend, Flanders, formerly in Dumfries, testament, 1793, Comm. Dumfries. [NRS]

JOHNSTON, CHRISTOPHER, born 1724, died April 1771 in Dumfries. [Dalton MI, Dumfries-shire]

JOHNSTON, DAVID, an inn-keeper, was admitted as a burgess of Dumfries in 1776. [DBR]; testament, 1798, Comm. Dumfries. [NRS]

JOHNSTON, ELIZABETH, daughter of George Johnston, a merchant in Dumfries, a deed, 1715. [NRS.RD2.105.127]

JOHNSTON, FRANCIS, arrived in Dumfries from Ireland in 1690. [NRS.CH2.537.15.1/29]

JOHNSTON, FRANCIS, a merchant bailie in Dumfries, testaments, 1752, 1758, Comm. Dumfries. [NRS]

JOHNSTON, GEORGE, a merchant in Dumfries, 1682. [NRS.GD78.166/186]; testaments, 1694, 1705,1706, Comm. Dumfries. [NRS]

JOHNSTON, GEORGE, son of George Johnston, a merchant in Dumfries, a deed, 1715. [NRS.RD2.105.127]

JOHNSTONE, GEORGE, a cooper in Dumfries, was admitted as a burgess of Dumfries in 1757. [DBR]; 1786. [NRS.CS51.Letterbook]

JOHNSTON, GEORGE, a broker, was admitted as a burgess of Dumfries in 1785. [DBR]

JOHNSTON, Dr GEORGE MILLIGAN, a surgeon in Charleston, South Carolina, a Loyalist in 1776, died 1799 in Dumfries. [TNA.AP12.50.239] [AJ. 2671]

JOHNSTON, HERBERT, a merchant burgess in Dumfries, testament, 1626, Comm. Dumfries. [NRS]

JOHNSTON, ISOBEL, relict of William Finglass a bailie of Dumfries, testament, 1721, Comm. Dumfries. [NRS]

JOHNSTON, JAMES, a surgeon in Dumfries, testament, 1734, Comm. Dumfries. [NRS]

JOHNSTON, JAMES, a skinner, was admitted as a burgess of Dumfries in 1735. [DBR]

JOHNSTON, JAMES, a smith, was admitted as a burgess of Dumfries in 1744. [DBR]

JOHNSTON, JAMES, a joiner, was admitted as a burgess of Dumfries in 1762. [DBR]

JOHNSTON, JAMES, a baker, was admitted as a burgess of Dumfries in 1786. [DBR]; in Dumfries, 1791. [NRS.CS235.SEQN.1J.1.3

JOHNSTON, JAMES, an innkeeper in Dumfries, was admitted as a burgess of Dumfries in 1770. [DBR]; sequestration, 1798. [NRS.D1.127/1.208/273]

JOHNSTON, JAMES, and David Anderson, merchants in Dumfries, sequestration, 1804. [NRS.DI.127/1.218/208]

JOHNSTON, JEAN, spouse to James Wilson a mariner at the port of Dumfries, testament, 1799, Comm. Dumfries. [NRS]

JOHNSTON, JOHN, a burgess of Dumfries, accused of liberating a prisoner from Dumfries Prison, 1600. [RPCS.VI.636]

JOHNSTON, JOHN, a merchant in Dumfries, trading with La Rochelle, France, in 1631. [NRS.AC7.2.386]

JOHNSTON, JOHN, a merchant in Dumfries, a witness, 1688. [RPCS.XIII. 284]; testament [missing] 1710, Comm. Dumfries. [NRS]

JOHNSTON, JOHN, and family, arrived in Dumfries from Ireland in 1690. [NRS.CH2.537.15.1/27]

JOHNSTON, JOHN, the elder, a merchant in Dumfries, a deed, 1715. [NRS.RD2.105.351]

JOHNSTON, JOHN, a merchant baillie of Dumfries, 1733. [NRS.GD219.216]

JOHNSTON, JOHN, a smith, was admitted as a burgess of Dumfries in 1762. [DBR]

JOHNSTON, JOHN, a smith, was admitted as a burgess of Dumfries in 1777. [DBR]

JOHNSTON, JOHN, a merchant in Dumfries, sequestration, 1792. [NRS.D1.127/1.207/433]

JOHNSTON, JOHN, a resident of Dumfries and a Captain-Lieutenant of the Marines, testaments, 1795, 1797, Comm. Dumfries. [NRS]

JOHNSTON, JOHN, born 1766, died 19 May 1836, father of William Johnston born 1803, died on St Bartholemew's, West Indies, 21 November 1827. [St Michael's MI, Dumfries]

JOHNSTON, JOSEPH, a surgeon in Dumfries, testaments, 1765, 1778, Comm. Dumfries. [NRS]

JOHNSTON, JOSEPH, a tailor in Dumfries, 1785. [NRS.CS271.42982]

JOHNSTON, MARGARET, spouse of John Graham a merchant bailie of Dumfries, heir to her father Francis Johnston a merchant there, in 1742, [NRS.S/H]; a disposition, 1764. [NRS.CS231.G2.32]

JOHNSTON, MARY, arrived in Dumfries from Ireland in 1690.
[NRS.CH2.537.15.1/35]

JOHNSTON, MATTHEW, master of the Mally of Dumfries was captured by an American privateer when bound for Nova Scotia in 1776 but was later liberated by the Royal Navy in 1777. [NRS.AC7.60]

JOHNSTON, Captain ROBERT, a merchant bailie of Dumfries, and his eldest son Robert Johnston of Kelton, deeds, 1691. [NRS.RD2.74.291; RD4.68.188]; titles, 1689-1718. [NRS.GD10.166]; Provost of Dumfries, 1706. [NRS.AC13.5.20]; Provost of Dumfries, deeds, 1702/1715. [NRS.RD4.90.154; RD2.105.127]

JOHNSTON, ROBERT, of Kelton, born 1643, Provost and MP, died 3 November 1715. [St Michael's MI]; see charter of 1707. [EUL.LC.3036]

JOHNSTON, ROBERT, a tide-waiter, was admitted as a burgess of Dumfries in 1750. [DBR]

JOHNSTON, ROBERT, a nailer, was admitted as a burgess of Dumfries in 1754. [DBR]

JOHNSTONE, ROBERT, a chapman in Dumfries, testament, 1781, 1782,1785, Comm. Dumfries. [NRS]

JOHNSTONE, ROBERT, a gunsmith, was admitted as a burgess of Dumfries in 1798. [DBR]

JOHNSTONE, THOMAS, master of the Providence of Dumfries, 1689. [NRS.E72.6.13]

JOHNSTON, WALTER, a saddler, was admitted as a burgess of Dumfries in 1739. [DBR]

JOHNSTON, WALTER, a joiner in Dumfries, testament, 1794, Comm. Dumfries. [NRS]

JOHNSTON, WILLIAM, a merchant burgess of Dumfries, accused of liberating a prisoner from Dumfries Prison, 1600. [RPCS.VI.636]

JOHNSTON, WILLIAM, master of the Kirkconnell of Dumfries, 1721. [NRS.AC9.764][to Virginia in 1714 and in 1715, see DGA,G74.19A/10]

JOHNSTON, WILLIAM, eldest son of Joseph Johnston a surgeon in Dumfries, a testament, 1747, Comm. Dumfries. [NRS]

JOHNSTON, WILLIAM, a shipmaster, was admitted as a burgess of Dumfries in 1751. [DBR]

JOHNSTON, WILLIAM, jr., a smith, was admitted as a burgess of Dumfries in 1754. [DBR]

JOHNSTON, WILLIAM, a tailor, was admitted as a burgess of Dumfries in 1795. [DBR]

JOHNSTON, WILLIAM, born 1803, died 21 November 1827 in St Bartholemew, West Indies. [St Michael's MI, Dumfries]J

JOHNSTON, WINIFRED, relict of John Wilson an Excise officer in Dumfries, testament, 1795, Comm. Dumfries. [NRS]

KA, PATRICK, residing in Dumfries, suspected of Catholicism, 1601. [RPCS.VI.312]

KA, ROBERT, residing in Dumfries, suspected of Catholicism, 1601. [RPCS.VI.312]

KAE, CHRISTOPHER, a workman in Dumfries, testament, 1625, Comm. Dumfries. [NRS]

KAILLY, DAVID, an inn-keeper, was admitted as a burgess of Dumfries in 1744, [DBR]

KEIR, JAMES, in Dumfries, 1691. [RPCS.XV1.62]

KELLOCK, MARION, spouse to Simon Pickersgill a clothier burgess of Dumfries, testament, 1681, Comm. Dumfries. [NRS]

KEMP, ROBERT, a joiner, was admitted as a burgess of Dumfries in 1770. [DBR]

KENNAN, JEAN, wife of John Wallace, a merchant in Dumfries, versus William Carruthers, a merchant in Dumfries, and Robert Kennan, a merchant in Virginia, 25 February 1769. [NRS.CS16.1.134]

KENNAN, JOHN, an innkeeper, was admitted as a burgess of Dumfries in 1758. [DBR]

KENNAN, ROBERT, a merchant from Dumfries, settled in Virginia 1769, died in Petersburg, Va., 1807. [NRS.CS16.1.134][Raleigh Register.23.7.1807]

KENNEDY, ANDREW, master of the St Andrew of Dumfries arrived in Virginia on 17 August 1752. [VaGaz.90]; trading between Dumfries, Dieppe and Virginia, 1750-1754, [AJ.157][VaGaz.91][TDG,34.50][NRS.E504.9.2]; son of John Kennedy of Knockgray, Galloway, testament, 10 October 1765, Commissariat of Edinburgh. [NRS]

KENNEDY, DAVID, a wright, was admitted as a burgess of Dumfries in 1754. [DBR]

KENNEDY, GEORGE, a merchant in Dumfries, 1622. [NRS.E71.10.5]

KENNEDY, JAMES, a glover and skinner in Dumfries, was admitted as a burgess of Dumfries in 1739, [DBR]; 1790. [NRS.CS271.48129]

KENNEDY, JAMES, a glover, was admitted as a burgess of Dumfries in 1759. [DBR]

KENNEDY, WILLIAM, a tobacconist in Dumfries, 1786. [NRS.CE51.Letterbook]

KENNOWAY, JAMES, a tailor burgess of Dumfries, 1601. [RPCS.VI.263]

KERR, ALEXANDER, schoolmaster of Dumfries, testament, 23 December 1723, Commissariat of Dumfries. [NRS]

KERR, ALEXANDER, a weaver, was admitted as a burgess of Dumfries in 1765. [DBR]

KERR, GEORGE, a merchant in Dumfries, and Violet, daughter of John Lanrick of Ladylands, a marriage contract, 1736. [NRS.RH8.886]

KERR, JAMES, born 1754 in Dumfries, emigrated to New York, a Loyalist officer, moved to Parrsboro, Nova Scotia, died 6 June 1830 in Amherst, Nova Scotia.[TNA.AO12.85.59]

KERR, JAMES, a merchant, was admitted as a burgess of Dumfries in 1799. [DBR]

KERR, ROBERT, a writer in Dumfries, 1727. [NRS.AC9.1015]

KERR, ROBERT, a shoemaker, was admitted as a burgess of Dumfries in 1764. [DBR]

KERR, THOMAS, a merchant in Dumfries, testament, 1795, Comm. Dumfries. [NRS]

KERR, WILLIAM, a shoemaker, was admitted as a burgess of Dumfries in 1739, [DBR]

KESSOCK, ALEXANDER, a drover in Dumfries, an inhibition, 1799. [NRS.D1.127/1.213/722]

KEY, JOHN, a tobacconist in Dumfries, was admitted as a burgess of Dumfries in 1752. [DBR]; 1786. [NRS.CE51.Letterbook]

KINCAID, JOHN, a Covenanter imprisoned in Dumfries Tolbooth, transported to East New Jersey in 1685. [RPCS.XI.154]

KINGHORN, ANDREW, a millwright in Dumfries, testament, 1783, Comm. Dumfries. [NRS]

KIRKCONNELL, WILLIAM, a mason in Dumfries, testament, 1741, Comm. Dumfries. [NRS]

KIRKPATRICK, CHARLES, a merchant, was admitted as a burgess of Dumfries in 1752. [DBR]

KIRKPATRICK, DANIEL, a saddler burgess of Dumfries, accused of liberating a prisoner from Dumfries Prison, 1600. [RPCS.VI.636]

KIRKPATRICK, DANIEL, a shoemaker, was admitted as a burgess of Dumfries in 1766. [DBR]

KIRKPATRICK, EDWARD, a cordiner at the Bridgend of Dumfries, testament, 1675, Comm. Dumfries. [NRS]

KIRKPATRICK, EDWARD, eldest son of the late Edward Kirkpatrick, a cordiner at the Bridgend of Dumfries, testament, 1679, Comm. Dumfries. [NRS]

KIRKPATRICK, JOHN, a merchant burgess of Dumfries, testament, 1600, Commissary of Edinburgh. [NRS]

KIRKPATRICK, JOHN, a wigmaker in Dumfries, son of Roger Kirkpatrick in Lochside of Auldgirth, 1741. [NRS.GD19.188]

KIRKPATRICK, JOSEPH, a joiner in Dumfries, was admitted as a burgess of Dumfries in 1739, [DBR]; testament, 1756, Comm. Dumfries. [NRS]

KIRKPATRICK, ROBERT, Provost of Dumfries, 1614. [NRS.GD10.703-5]

KIRKPATRICK, ROGER, a bailie burgess of Dumfries, accused of liberating a prisoner from Dumfries Prison, 1600. [RPCS.VI.636]

KIRKPATRICK, ROGER, a merchant burgess of Dumfries, a deed, 1619. [NRS.GD10.713]

KIRKPATRICK, RODGER, Provost and burgess of Dumfries, testament, 1626, Comm. Dumfries. [NRS]

KIRKPATRICK, SAMUEL, from Dumfries, a member of the Scots Charitable Society of Boston in 1769. [NEHGS/SCS]

KIRKPATRICK, THOMAS, in Dumfries, husband of Janet Anderson, testament, 1641, Comm. Dumfries. [NRS]

KIRKPATRICK, THOMAS, a merchant in Dumfries, testaments, 1747, 1752, Comm. Dumfries. [NRS]

KIRKPATRICK, THOMAS, a tailor, was admitted as a burgess of Dumfries in 1759. [DBR]

KIRKPATRICK, THOMAS, jr., a tailor, was admitted as a burgess of Dumfries in 1759. [DBR]

KIRKPATRICK, WILLIAM, a merchant in Dumfries, was admitted as a burgess of Dumfries in 1739, [DBR]; trading with Virginia 1748, and with Prince Edward Island in 1780; versus John Miller in Prince Edward Island, 11 August 1780. [NRS. E504.92; CS16.1.181]; merchant bailie in Dumfries, testament, 20 May 1793, Comm. Dumfries. [NRS]; born 1709, died April 1782. [St Michael's MI]

KIRKPATRICK, WILLIAM, jr., a merchant, was admitted as a burgess of Dumfries in 1761. [DBR]

KIRKPATRICK, WILLIAM, of Conbeath, Customs surveyor at the port of Dumfries, testaments, 1788, 1789, Comm. Dumfries. [NRS]

KIRKPATRICK, WILLIAM, a tobacconist in Dumfries, 1786.
[NRS.CE51.Letterbook]

KIRKPATRICK and CURRIE, merchants in Dumfries, trading with Nova
Scotia and New York in 1776. [NRS.AC7.60]

LAIDLAW, WILLIAM, a gardener, was admitted as a burgess of Dumfries in
1765, [DBR]

LAIDLAW, WILLIAM, a writer, was admitted as a burgess of Dumfries in
1791, [DBR]

LAIDLAY, THOMAS, a shopkeeper, was admitted as a burgess of Dumfries in
1778, [DBR]

LAMB, JOHN, a goldsmith burgess of Dumfries, 1601. [RPCS.VI.263]

LANRICK, JOHN, of Torrery, 1707, [EUL/LC.3036]; town clerk of Dumfries,
deeds, 1714-1716. [NRS.RH8.931]; testament, 28 October 1754, Comm.
Dumfries. [NRS]

LARMONT, JOHN, a shopkeeper, was admitted as a burgess of Dumfries in
1773, [DBR]

LARMONT, THOMAS, a shopkeeper, was admitted as a burgess of Dumfries
in 1775, [DBR]

LAUDER, ROBERT, a writer in Dumfries, and his wife Sophia Craik, a sasine,
9 August 1710. [NRS.RS23.7.495]

LAWITER, JOHN, a shopkeeper, was admitted as a burgess of Dumfries in
1786, [DBR]

LAWRIE, AGNES, spouse of David Bell a merchant burgess of Dumfries,
testament, 1630, Comm. Dumfries. [NRS]

LAWRIE, ALEXANDER, a labourer from Dumfries, emigrated via Bristol to
Virginia in 1658. [BRO.04220]

LAWRIE, JOHN, in Dumfries, grandfather and tutor to William Lawrie, son of
the deceased William Lawrie a merchant burgess of Dumfries, an assignation,
1634. [NRS.GD6.1907]

LAWRIE, STEPHEN, a merchant burgess of Dumfries, 1619.
[NRS.GD39.1.196]

LAWRIE, WILLIAM, a merchant burgess of Dumfries, testament, 1630, Comm
Dumfries. [NRS]

LAWRIE, WILLIAM, a merchant burgess of Dumfries, horning, 1633.
[NRS.GD6.1904]

LAWRIE, WILLIAM, a slater burgess of Dumfries, process of damages for
wrongful imprisonment, 28 June 1731. [NRS.CC8.6.246]

LAWRIE, WILLIAM, a writer in Dumfries, testament,1744, Comm. Dumfries.
[NRS]

LAWRIE, WILLIAM, in Dumfries, testament, 1780, Comm. Dumfries. [NRS]

LAWSON, AGNES, spouse to William Palmer a merchant in Dumfries,
testament, 1680, Comm. Dumfries. [NRS]

LAWSON, ELIZABETH, a shopkeeper in Dumfries, testament, 1734, Comm.
Dumfries. [NRS]

LAWSON, HUGH, a merchant in Dumfries, testament, 1721, Comm. Dumfries.
[NRS]

LAWSON, HUGH, was admitted as a burgess of Dumfries in 1738, [DBR]; a
merchant in Dumfries, versus Thomas Kirkpatrick, a merchant in Alexandria,
Virginia, 24 February 1779; trading with Va. 1782. [NRS.CS16.1.175;
CS17.1.1]

LAWSON, JOHN, a merchant, was admitted as a burgess of Dumfries in 1762,
[DBR]

LAWSON, MARGARET, daughter of the deceased Hugh Lawson a merchant
in Dumfries, testament, 1747, Comm. Dumfries. [NRS]

LAWSON, MARY, relict of Walter Owens, an innkeeper in Dumfries,
testament, 1799, Comm. Dumfries. [NRS]

LAWSON, MICHAEL, a merchant in Dumfries, was admitted as a merchant
burgess of Dumfries in 1740, [DBR]; testament, 1741, Comm. Dumfries. [NRS]

LAWSON, ROBERT, a merchant in Dumfries, testament, 1675, Comm. Dumfries. [NRS]

LAWSON, ROBERT, son of Robert Lawson of Knockhorrock, [1728-1800], and his wife Helen Hannah, died in St Kitts aged 24. [St Michael's MI, Dumfries]

LAWSON, ROBERT, a shopkeeper, was admitted as a burgess of Dumfries in 1786, [DBR]

LAWSON, WILLIAM, a tailor in Dumfries, testament,1682, Comm. Dumfries. [NRS]

LAWSON, WILLIAM, was admitted as a burgess of Dumfries in 1776, [DBR]; a merchant in Dumfries, versus Thomas Kirkpatrick, a merchant in Alexandria, Virginia, 23 January 1782. [NRS.CS17.1.1]

LAWSON, ..., a ship-owner in Dumfries, 1786. [NRS.CE51.Letterbook]

LAWSON, JARDINE, and Company, merchants in Dumfries, 1755. [NRS.GD18.5749]

LEARMONT, ADAM, a merchant in Dumfries, testament,1750, Comm. Dumfries. [NRS]

LECKIE, MARGARET, born 1696, spouse of James Mitchelson, died 14 January 1781. [S Michael's MI, Dumfries]

LEWARS, JANET, spouse to Alexander Fairbairn, a locksmith burgess of Dumfries, testament,1679, Comm. Dumfries. [NRS]

LEWARS, JOHN, a merchant burgess of Dumfries, testament, 1679, Comm. Dumfries. [NRS]

LEWARS, JOHN, Excise supervisor in Dumfries, testament, 1789, Comm. Dumfries. [NRS]

LEWARS, THOMAS, a merchant in Dumfries, a deed, 1715. [NRS.RD2.104.459]

LIGHTBODY, ISABEL, in Dumfries, widow of John Hyslop, testament, 1793, Comm. Dumfries. [NRS]

LIN, PATRICK, born 1687, graduated MA from Edinburgh University, minister of St Michael's, Dumfries, from 1715 until his death 1 August 1731, Husband of Alison Chalmers. [F.2.268]; testament, 1733, Comm. Dumfries. [NRS]

LINDSAY, EDWARD, a merchant burgess of Dumfries, testament, 1674, Comm. Dumfries. [NRS]

LINDSAY, JOHN, a shopkeeper, was admitted as a burgess of Dumfries in 1779, [DBR]

LINDSAY, ROBERT, a shopkeeper, was admitted as a burgess of Dumfries in 1784, [DBR]

LISLE, JOHN, a tobacconist in Dumfries, 1786. [NRS.CE51.Letterbook]

LITSTER, ROBERT, a shopkeeper, was admitted as a burgess of Dumfries in 1783, [DBR]

LITSTER, WILLIAM, a merchant in Dumfries, testaments, 1785, 1786, Comm. Dumfries. [NRS]

LITSTER, ROBERT, a tailor in Dumfries, 1785. [NRS.CS271.42982]

LITTLE, ELIZABETH, relict of William Norvell late baker in Dumfries, testaments, 1786, 1788, Comm. Dumfries. [NRS]

LITTLE, ..., master of the Murray of Dumfries arrived in Leith from Veere, Zealand, on 25 September 1755. [AJ.403]

LIVINGSTON, JOHN, a shopkeeper, was admitted as a burgess of Dumfries in 1775, [DBR]

LIVINGSTON, JOHN, a shopkeeper, was admitted as a burgess of Dumfries in 1785, [DBR]

LIVINGSTON, ROBERT, a weaver, was admitted as a burgess of Dumfries in 1759, [DBR]

LOCHEAD, GABRIEL, a baxter, was admitted as a burgess of Dumfries in 1754, [DBR]

LOCKE, JOHN, a tobacconist, was admitted as a burgess of Dumfries in 1766, [DBR]; at Bridgend of Dumfries, 1786. [NRS.CE51.Letterbook]

LOCKERT, THOMAS, a merchant in Dumfries, testament, 1685, Comm. Dumfries. [NRS]

LOGAN, JOHN, jailor in Dumfries, and his wife Mary Linton, testament, 10 October 1685, Comm. Dumfries. [NRS]; accused of allowing a prisoner to escape from Dumfries Tolbooth in 1683. [RPCS.VIII.152]

LOGAN, WILLIAM, a merchant in Dumfries, testament, 1744, Comm. Dumfries. [NRS]

LOOKUP, ALEXANDER, was admitted as a burgess of Dumfries in 1784, [DBR]; a glover and skinner in Dumfries, 1790. [NRS.CS271.36035]

LOOKUP, WILLIAM, a shopkeeper, was admitted as a burgess of Dumfries in 1774, [DBR]

LORIMER, JAMES, a coppersmith, was admitted as a burgess of Dumfries in 1741, [DBR]

LORIMER, WILLIAM, a shop-keeper, was admitted as a burgess of Dumfries in 1768, [DBR]

LOTHIAN, BRIDGET, relict of George Lothian of Staffold, residing in Dumfries, testament, 1743, Comm. Dumfries. [NRS]

LOTHIAN, RICHARD, of Staffold, Cumberland, a resident of Dumfries, testaments, 1787, 1793, 1794, Comm. Dumfries. [NRS]

LOURIE, JAMES, a merchant burgess of Dumfries, testament, 1675, Comm. Dumfries. [NRS]

LOWDEN, WILLIAM, master of the Mally of Dumfries bound for Halifax, Nova Scotia, in April 1776. [NRS.E504.21.4; AC7.60]

LOWRIE, ANNE, relict of George Sharp a merchant burgess of Dumfries, a marriage contract with Alexander Douglas, a Writer to the Signet, 1642. [NRS.GD77.17.4]

LOWRIE, STEVEN, a merchant in Dumfries, trading with Flanders in 1622. [NAS.E71.10.5]

LYLE, JOHN, a shopkeeper, was admitted as a burgess of Dumfries in 1784, [DBR]

LYN, FERGUS, a merchant in Dumfries, 1621. [NAS.E71.10.5]

LYON, JAMES, a bricklayer, was admitted as a burgess of Dumfries in 1754, [DBR]

MCBRAIR, DAVID, in Dumfries, husband of Jean Douglas, a deed, 1702. [NRS.RD4.90.1065]

MCBRAIR, ROBERT, a messenger in Dumfries, eldest son and heir to the late Robert McBrair a messenger in Dumfries, [EUL.LC3036]; a deed, 1702, [NRS.RD2.86.2.183]; testaments, 1736, 1737, 1755, and 1759, Comm. Dumfries. [NRS]

MCBRAIR, ROBERT, of Almegle, elected Provost of Dumfries, 1599. [RPCS.VI.39]

MCBRAIR, ROBERT, a messenger in Dumfries, a deed, 1691. [NRS.RD4.68.12]; testament [missing] 1714, Comm. Dumfries. [NRS]

MCBRAIR, THOMAS, a merchant burgess of Dumfries, testament, 1642, Comm. Dumfries. [NRS]

MCBRIDE, JOHN, master of the Scotia of Dumfries a smuggler captured by a Customs cutter on 17 January 1789. [AJ.2142]

MCBURNE, THOMAS, residing in Dumfries, suspected of Catholicism, 1601. [RPCS.VI.312]

MCBURNIE, JANET, spouse to Wilkaine Irving a merchant burgess of Dumfries, testament, 1629, Comm. Dumfries. [NRS]

MCBURNIE, JOHN, a shoemaker in Dumfries, testament, 1689, Comm. Dumfries. [NRS]

MCBURNIE, MARION, relict of Thomas Goldie a merchant burgess of Dumfries, testament, 1638, Comm. Dumfries. [NRS]

MCBURNIE, MARY, relict of George Irving a merchant in Dumfries, testament, 1678, Comm. Dumfries. [NRS]

MCBURNIE, ROBERT, a notary burgess of Dumfries, testament, 1658, Comm. Dumfries. [NRS]

MCBURNIE, WILLIAM, a merchant burgess of Dumfries, testament, 1658, Comm. Dumfries. [NRS]

MCCALLUM, WILLIAM, a merchant in Dumfries, a deed, 1714. [NRS.RD2.103.2.573]

MCCARTNEY, ANDREW, a gardener in Dumfries, was admitted as a burgess of Dumfries in 1746. [DBR]; testament, 1793, Comm. Dumfries. [NRS]

MCCASKIE, JAMES, a tobacconist in Dumfries, 1727. [NRS.AC9.1015]

MCCASKIE, JAMES, jr., a merchant. was admitted as a burgess of Dumfries in 1761. [DBR]

MCCASKIE, ROBERT, a shopkeeper, was admitted as a burgess of Dumfries in 1765. [DBR]

MCCAUGLINE, JAMES, was admitted as a burgess of Dumfries in 1798. [DBR]

MCCAULL, AGNES, relict of Edward Paterson a merchant in Dumfries, testament [missing] 1710, Comm. Dumfries. [NRS]

MCCLAMEROCH, MARGARET, relict of John Mulligan merchant in Dumfries, a deed, 1691. [NRS.RD2.73.514]

MCCLAUCHRY, WILLIAM, a weaver, was admitted as a burgess of Dumfries in 1747. [DBR]

MCCLELLAN, JOHN, a merchant, was admitted as a burgess of Dumfries in 1766. [DBR]

MCCLELLAN, MARGARET, relict of James Brown a writer in Dumfries, testament, 1764, Comm. Dumfries. [NRS]

MCCLELLAN, THOMAS, a wright, was admitted as a burgess of Dumfries in 1738. [DBR]

MCCLEN, GILBERT, a merchant in Dumfries, 1621. [NRS.E71.10.5]

MCCONNOCHIE, ROBERT, a tobacconist in Dumfries, 1786. [NRS.CE51.Letterbook]

MCCORNOCK, HUGH, born 1760, a merchant in Dumfries, died 21 January 1800. [St Michael's MI, Dumfries]

MCCORNOCK, WILLIAM, a merchant in Dumfries, testaments, 1731, 1732, Comm. Dumfries. [NRS]

MCCORNOCK, WILLIAM, a writer in Dumfries, testament, 1769, Comm. Dumfries. [NRS]

MCCORNOCK, WILLIAM, a merchant in Dumfries, a disposition, 1769. [NRS.GD19.159]

MCCOURTIE, ALEXANDER, a merchant, was admitted as a burgess of Dumfries in 1754. [DBR]

MCCREERY, ROBERT, a merchant in Dumfries, husband of Janet Verner, deeds, 1714. [NRS.RD2.103.2.550; RD2.54.257.126]

MCCRERIE, CATHERINE, spouse to John Gibson a flesher burgess of Dumfries, testament, 1628, Comm. Dumfries. [NRS]

MCCRERIE, ELIZABETH, a widow in Dumfries, testament, 1656, Comm. Dumfries. [NRS]

MCCULLOCH, DAVID, in Dumfries, bills of exchange, 1711-1716. [NRS.GD180.299]

MCCULLOCH, JAMES, from Dumfries, a member of the Scots Charitable Society of Boston in 1747. [NEHGS/SCSpp]

MCCULLOCH, JAMES, born 1727, a labourer from Dumfries, emigrated aboard the Lovely Nelly to Prince Edward Island in 1775. [TNA.47.12]

MACDOWELL, WILLIAM, of Gategill, an accountant in the Bank of Scotland in Dumfries, testaments, 1789, 1792, 1794, and 1795, Comm. Dumfries. [NRS]; an accountant in Dumfries, 1786. [NRS.CE51.Letterbook]

MACFARLANE, DOUGALL, a merchant burgess of Dumfries, 1727. [NRS.AC9.1037]; dead by 1734. [NRS.CS228.A2/7]; testaments, 1730, 1731, 1735, and 1735, Comm. Dumfries. [NRS]

MCGACHIE, MARGARET, born 1717, wife of Provost Ebenezer Hepburn, died 19 March 1765. [St Michael's MI, Dumfries]

MCGEORGE, JAMES, of Nether Larg, residing in Dumfries, testament, 1748, Comm. Dumfries. [NRS]

MCGEORGE, JOHN, a shopkeeper, was admitted as a burgess of Dumfries in 1769. [DBR]; a tobacconist in Dumfries, 1786. [NRS.CE51.Letterbook]

MCGEORGE, WILLIAM, clerk to the Fleshers of Dumfries, 1679. [NRS]

MCGHIE, JAMES, an innkeeper, was admitted as a burgess of Dumfries in 1799. [DBR]

MCGHIE, JOHN, residing in Dumfries, suspected of Catholicism, 1601. [RPCS.VI.312]

MCGHIE, S., a painter, was admitted as a burgess of Dumfries in 1759. [DBR]

MCGHIE, WILLIAM, a glazier in Dumfries, a Jacobite in 1745-1746, a prisoner. [LPR.144]

MCGOWAN, JAMES, a merchant in Dumfries, 1622. [NRS.E71.10.5]

MCGOWAN, MARGARET, born 1675, wife of William Copland of Colliston, died 17 September 1730. [St Michael's MI, Dumfries]

MCGOWN, AGNES, in Dumfries, relict of Robert Corsan, and their son Robert Corsan, a disposition, 1772. [NRS.CS226.G4.19]

MCGOWN, ALEXANDER, a merchant burgess of Dumfries, testaments, 1678, 1680, Comm. Dumfries. [NRS]

MCGOUNE, ALEXANDER, in Dumfries, a letter, 1731. [NRS.GD47.460]

MCGOUNE, JOHN, a merchant in Dumfries, 1675. [NRS.GD128.16.28]

MCGOWN, MARION, a widow in Dumfries, testament, 1677, Comm. Dumfries. [NRS]

MCGOWN, MARION, relict of William Welsh a merchant in Dumfries, testament [missing] 1699, Comm. Dumfries. [NRS]

MCGOWAN, JAMES, an innkeeper, was admitted as a burgess of Dumfries in 1798. [DBR]

MCGUFFOCK, ROBERT, a shoemaker, was admitted as a burgess of Dumfries in 1738. [DBR]

MCHARG, JOHN, with his wife and family, arrived in Dumfries from Ireland in 1690. [NRS.CH2.537.15.1/36]

MCILREEN, BENJAMIN, a weaver, was admitted as a burgess of Dumfries in 1738. [DBR]

MCILROY, JOHN, a tailor, was admitted as a burgess of Dumfries in 1740. [DBR]

MCILROY, WILLIAM, a tailor, was admitted as a burgess of Dumfries in 1769. [DBR]

MCILWAYLL, DAVID, a merchant burgess of Dumfries, testament, 1661, Comm. Dumfries. [NRS]

MCINTOSH, ROBERT, an advocate, was admitted as a burgess of Dumfries in 1762. [DBR]

MCJARROW, WILLIAM, in Dumfries, a deed, 1715. [NRS.RD2.105.127]

MCJORE, WILLIAM, schoolmaster of Dumfries, husband of Katherine Copland, deeds, 1664-1667. [NRS.RD2.12.571; RD2.18.600]

MCKAY, ROBERT, born 1790, son of James McKay and his wife Ann Ferguson, [171-1803], died 1821 in Concord, Tobago. [Dumfries MI]

MCKENNEL, ..., a merchant in Dumfries, 1786. [NAS.CE51.Letterbook]

MCKENZIE, DONALD, a glover in Dumfries, testament, 1686, Comm. Dumfries. [NRS]

MCKENZIE, of Netherwood, GEORGE, a writer in Dumfries, sasines, 1773-1780. [NRS.RS23.XXI.415; XXII.81/225]

MCKENZIE, JOHN, was admitted as a burgess of Dumfries in 1764. [DBR]; conjunct town clerk of Dumfries, testaments, 1784, 1786, 1789, 1790, and 1791, Comm. Dumfries. [NRS]

MCKENZIE, SIMON, a writer in Dumfries, a sasine, 1778. [NRS.RS23.XXII. 109]

MCKIE, ALEXANDER, a surgeon, was admitted as a burgess of Dumfries in 1742. [DBR]

MCKIE, HOB, a burgess of Dumfries, his wife Agnes Maxwell, and son James McKie, petitioned the Privy Council of Scotland 10 July 1599. [RPCS.VI.11]

MACKIE, HUGH, master of the <u>Adventure of Dumfries</u>, 1688, and of the <u>Margaret of Dumfries</u>, 1689. [NRS.E72.6.11-15]

MCKIE, JAMES, a shoemaker, was admitted as a burgess of Dumfries in 1757. [DBR]

MCKIE, JAMES, a merchant in Dumfries, testament, 1773, Comm. Dumfries. [NRS]

MCKIE, ISOBEL, daughter of John McKie, a writer in Dumfries, and spouse of David Johnston of the Chatham division of the Marines, a sasine, 1772. [NRS.RS23.XXI.224]

MCKIE, JOHN, a writer in Dumfries, husband of Mary Hodgson, sasines, 1770s. [NRS.RS23.XX.195-196; XXI.224/412]

MCKIE, MARION, in Dumfries, testament, 1674, Comm. Dumfries. [NRS]

MCKIE, WILLIAM, a horse-hirer, was admitted as a burgess of Dumfries in 1742. [DBR]

MCKIE, WILLIAM, a workman, was admitted as a burgess of Dumfries in 1750. [DBR]

MCKILL, MATTHEW, a tailor, was admitted as a burgess of Dumfries in 1750. [DBR]

MCKILL, ROBERT, a tailor, was admitted as a burgess of Dumfries in 1759. [DBR]

MCKINNELL, JAMES, a merchant, was admitted as a burgess of Dumfries in 1743. [DBR]

MCKINNELL, JAMES, a shoemaker, was admitted as a burgess of Dumfries in 1743. [DBR]

MCKINNELL, JANET, daughter of the deceased William McKinnell late merchant in Dumfries, testament, 1787, Comm. Dumfries. [NRS]

MCKINNELL, JOHN, a shoemaker, was admitted as a burgess of Dumfries in 1750. [DBR]

MCKINNELL, JOHN, of Glen, a brewer in Dumfries, testament, 1786, Comm. Dumfries. [NRS]

MCKINNELL, MARY, a mantua maker in Dumfries, a sasine, 1778. [NRS.RS23.39]

MCKINNELL, ROBERT, a nailer, was admitted as a burgess of Dumfries in 1754. [DBR]

MCKINNELL, ROBERT, late a farmer in Auchencreith, thereafter residing in Dumfries, testaments, 1778 and 1789, Comm. Dumfries. [NRS]

MCKINNELL, THOMAS, a merchant in Dumfries, testament, 1721, Comm. Dumfries. [NRS]

MCKINNELL, WILLIAM, late Deacon Convenor of Dumfries, testament, 1674, Comm. Dumfries. [NRS]

MCKINNELL, WILLIAM, son of the late William McKinnell Deacon Convenor of the Trades in Dumfries, testament, 1680, Comm. Dumfries. [NRS]

MCKINNELL, WILLIAM, a merchant, was admitted as a burgess of Dumfries in 1739. [DBR]; a sasine, 1761. [NRS.RS23.XIX.269]

MCKINSHE, GILBERT, a cordiner at the Bridgend of Dumfries, testament, 1628, Comm. Dumfries. [NRS]

MCKITTRICK, AGNES, daughter of James McKittrick a merchant in Dumfries, deeds, 1702. [NRS.RD3.100.240/253]

MCKITTRICK, ANNA, daughter of James McKittrick a merchant in Dumfries, deeds, 1702. [NRS.RD3.100.240/253]

MCKITTRICK, ELIZABETH, daughter of James McKittrick a merchant in Dumfries, deeds, 1702. [NRS.RD3.100.240/253]

MCKITRICK, ELIZABETH, relict of Stephen Irving bailie of Dumfries deeds, 1691, 1714. [NRS.RD2.73.53; RD4.67.947; RD 4.68.117; GD78.207]

MCKITTRICK, ISOBEL, daughter of James McKittrick a merchant in Dumfries, deeds, 1702. [NRS.RD3.100.240/253]

MCKITTRICK, JAMES, a merchant in Dumfries, husband of Isobel McGowan, parents of Isobel, Agnes, Anna, and Elizabeth, deeds, 1702/1714. [NRS.RD3.100.240; RD4.115.386]

MCKITTERICK, JOHN, son of William McKitterick in Bridgend, Dumfries, a rioter, transported to Maryland, 1771. [NRS.JC27.10.3][SM.33.497]

MCKITTERICK, WILLIAM, a merchant bailie of Dumfries, dead by 1631. [NRS.GD78.62]

MCKITTERICK, WILLIAM, a merchant burgess of Dumfries, writs, 1654-1655. [NRS.GD10.197]; late bailie of Dumfries, testament, 1678, Comm. Dumfries. [NRS]

MCKNO, JAMES, a jailer in Dumfries, accused of allowing a prisoner to escape from Dumfries Tolbooth in 1683. [RPCS.VIII.152]; aged 28, unmarried, burgh officer of Dumfries in 1687. [RPCS.XIII.169]

MCLAUGHLAN, ALAN, a bookseller, was admitted as a burgess of Dumfries in 1761. [DBR]; a bookseller in Dumfries, 1776. [NRS.CS228.B.6.]; sasines, 1760s. [NRS.RS23.XIX.404/405/464; XX.330]

MCLEAN, CHRISTIAN, spouse of John Black a merchant burgess of Dumfries, testaments, 1641, 1643, Comm. Dumfries. [NRS]

MCLEAN, GILBERT, a merchant burgess of Dumfries, testament, 1625, Comm. Dumfries. [NRS]

MCLEAN, WILLIAM, a shoemaker, was admitted as a burgess of Dumfries in 1745. [DBR]

MCLELLAN, CHARLES, a merchant in Dumfries, a deed, 1691. [NRS.RD3.75.412]

MCLELLAN, MARGARET, a Covenanter imprisoned in Dumfries Tolbooth, transported to East New Jersey in 1685. [RPCS.XI.154/291/292]

MCLELLAN, SAMUEL, a dyer in Dumfries, a deed, 1715. [NRS.RD4.117.334]

MCLELLAN, SAMUEL, a wright, was admitted as a burgess of Dumfries in 1770. [DBR]

MCMATH, JOHN, a shoemaker, was admitted as a burgess of Dumfries in 1742. [DBR]

MCMEEKAN, JEAN, widow of Robert McCandlish a mason at the Bridgend of Dumfries, testament, 1792, Comm. Dumfries. [NRS]

MCMICHAEL, JEAN, in Dumfries, testament, 1732, Comm. Dumfries. [NRS]

MCMICHAN, JAMES, a tobacconist at the Bridgend of Dumfries, 1786. [NRS.CE51.Letterbook]

MCMILLAN, JOHN, a merchant burgess of Dumfries, a sasine, 1635. [NRS.GD1.202.33]

MCMILLAN, JOHN, born 1769, son of Robert McMillan, [1749-1799], and his wife Margaret Donaldson, in Dumfries, died 7 October 1820 in Fayetteville, North Carolina.. [Dumfries MI] [Cross Creek MI, N.C.]

MCMILLAN, ROBERT, in Dumfries, testament, 1783, Comm. Dumfries. [NRS]

MCMILLAN, THOMAS, a merchant in Dumfries, trading with Flanders, 1622. [NRS.E71.10.5]

MCMIN, GEORGE, Deacon of the Smiths of Dumfries, 1733. [NRS.AC11.71]

MCMORRAN, EDWARD, a merchant, was admitted as a burgess of Dumfries in 1770. [DBR]; a merchant from Dumfries, settled in New York in 1774. [TNA.T47.12]

MCMORRIE, JAMES, a merchant burgess of Dumfries, testament, 1675, Comm. Dumfries. [NRS]

MCMURDO, ROBERT, a merchant and brewer in Dumfries, testament, 1790, Comm. Dumfries. [NRS]

MCMURDO, WILLIAM, a merchant, was admitted as a burgess of Dumfries in 1744. [DBR]

MCNAUGHT, ELIZABETH, relict of James Aitkin merchant at the Bridgend of Dumfries, sasine, 1711. [NRS.RS23.8.10]

MCNAUGHT, GEORGE, late Excise collector in Dumfries, testament, 1720, Comm. Dumfries. [NRS]

MCNAUGHT, JOHN, a burgess of Dumfries. testament, 1679, Comm. Dumfries. [NAS]

MCNAUGHT, JOHN, a merchant in Dumfries, husband of Agnes Corbet, court case, 1688. [RPCS.XIII.205]

MCNEISH, HELEN, spouse to Thomas Aiken a cordiner burgess of Dumfries, testament, 1676, Comm. Dumfries. [NRS]

MCNEISH, JOHN, a shoemaker, was admitted as a burgess of Dumfries in 1758. [DBR]

MCNEISH, WILLIAM, a shoemaker, was admitted as a burgess of Dumfries in 1750. [DBR]

MCNIGHT, JOHN, a Chelsea Pensioner residing in Dumfries, testament, 1798, Comm. Dumfries. [NRS]

MCNISH, JAMES, a tailor, was admitted as a burgess of Dumfries in 1738. [DBR]

MCNISH, WILLIAM, a tailor, was admitted as a burgess of Dumfries in 1764. [DBR]

MCNOE, JEAN, relict of John Gibson a merchant in Dumfries, testament, [missing] 1715, Comm. Dumfries. [NRS]

MCQUHONE, GILBERT, a merchant in Dumfries, trading with Flanders in 1622. [NRS.E71.10.5]

MCRAE, THOMAS, in Dumfries, testament, 1657, Comm. Dumfries. [NRS]

MCUMELL, ..., a deacon in Dumfries, 1691. [RPCS.XIII.62]

MCWHAE, GEORGE, in Dumfries, a deed, 1727. [NRS.GD10.158]

MCWHARRIE, JAMES, son of the late Thomas McWharrie a merchant in Dumfries, testament, 1688, Comm. Dumfries. [NRS]

MCWHARRIE, THOMAS, a dyer in Dumfries, husband of Mary Irving, a deed, 1702. [NRS.RD3.99.2.411]

MCWHIR, MUNGO, master of the Dumfries of Dumfries, 1786. [NRS.CE51.Letterbook]

MCWHIRTER, JAMES, a merchant, was admitted as a burgess of Dumfries in 1751. [DBR]; late a merchant in Dumfries, now in Dublin, adjudication, 1786. [NRS.D1.14.120.403]

MCWILLIAM, HUGH, a weaver, was admitted as a burgess of Dumfries in 1750. [DBR]

MCWILLIAM, JAMES, a merchant, was admitted as a burgess of Dumfries in 1765. [DBR]

MCWILLIAM, MARGARET, spouse to Charles Watson a shoemaker in Dumfries, testament, 1751, Comm. Dumfries. [NAS]

MABEN, DAVID, a merchant, was admitted as a burgess of Dumfries in 1771. [DBR]

MABAN, DAVID, a tanner in Dumfries, testament, 1785, Comm. Dumfries. [NAS]

MAIR, JANET, spouse to Thomas Dickson a cordiner in Dumfries, testament, 1682, Comm. Dumfries. [NAS]

MALCOLM, ALEXANDER, a merchant in Dumfries, deeds, 1714. [NRS.RD2.103.2.386, 573]

MALCOLM, ARCHIBALD, a writer, was admitted as a burgess of Dumfries in 1741. [DBR]; in Dumfries, a deed, 1772. [NRS.GD19.164]; conjunct town clerk of Dumfries, testament, 1795, Comm. Dumfries. [NAS]

MANDERSON, HUME, a tobacconist in Dumfries, 1786. [NRS.CE51.Letterbook]

MARCHBANK, ADAM, a weaver, was admitted as a burgess of Dumfries in 1741. [DBR]

MARSHALL, GEORGE, a vintner in Dumfries, testaments, 1774, 1778, Comm. Dumfries. [NRS]

MARSHALL, JOHN, bailie of Dumfries, 1601, [RPCS.VI.263]; a burgess of Dumfries, accused of liberating a prisoner from Dumfries Prison, 1600. [RPCS.VI.636]; a burgess of Dumfries, testament, 1626, Comm. Dumfries. [NRS]

MARTIN, AGNES, second daughter of John Martin late Convenor of the Trades of Dumfries, aged 24 and unmarried, a witness in 1687. [RPCS.XIII.170]

MARTIN, BALDWIN, a Customs officer at Dumfries, 1784. [NRS.CE51.2/3]

MARTIN, GEORGE, a merchant in Dumfries, sequestration, 1805. [NRS.DI.CCXIX.583]

MARTIN, HARBERT, a merchant in Dumfries, tutor to Christopher Irvine, a deed, 1714. [NRS.RD2.104.57]

MARTIN, JAMES, a merchant burgess of Dumfries, testament, 1638, Comm. Dumfries. [NAS]

MARTIN, JAMES, a glover in Dumfries, testaments [missing] 1700, 1713, Comm. Dumfries. [NRS]

MARTIN, JANET, a widow in Dumfries, testament, 1686, Comm. Dumfries. [NRS]

MARTIN, JOHN, a tailor burgess of Dumfries, 1601. [RPCS.VI.263]

MARTIN, JOHN, a writer in Dumfries, 1611. [CLC.1620]

MARTIN, JOHN, Deacon of the Fleshers of Dumfries, 1679. [DAC]

MARTIN, JOHN, treasurer of Dumfries in 1683, accused of allowing a prisoner to escape from Dumfries Tolbooth. [RPCS.VIII.152]

MARTIN, JOHN, son of John Martin, a merchant in Dumfries, a witness, 1687. [RPCS.XIII.156]

MARTIN, JOHN, a messenger in Dumfries, a deed, 1699. [NRS.RD2.83.562]

MARTINE, JOHN, the elder, a merchant in Dumfries, 1701. [NRS.RH9.4.147]

MARTIN, JOHN, of Kirkland, born 1658, a bailie of Dumfries, died 1 July 1714, father of William Martin, born 1716, died 29 April 1777. [St Michael's MI]; testament, [missing] 1715, Comm. Dumfries. [NRS]

MARTIN, JOHN, a merchant in Dumfries, 1707. [EUL.LC3036]

MARTIN, JOHN, a tobacconist in Dumfries, 1786. [NRS.CE51.Letterbook]

MARTIN, JOHN, a baxter in Dumfries, residing in the Old Flesh Market there, a decree, 1772. [NRS.CS229.M3.16]

MARTIN, JOHN, a messenger in Dumfries, a deed, 1699. [NRS.RD2.83.562]

MARTIN, JOHN, a baker, was admitted as a burgess of Dumfries in 1772. [DBR]

MARTIN, ROBERT, son of John Martin a flesher, was admitted as a journeyman to the Fleshers Incorporation of Dumfries on 30 September 1659. [DAC]

MARTIN, ROBERT, arrived in Dumfries from Ireland in 1690. [NRS.CH2.537.15.1/25]

MARTIN, THOMAS, a merchant burgess of Dumfries, testament, 1643, Comm. Dumfries. [NAS]

MARTIN, THOMAS, a writer in Dumfries, deeds, 1715. [NRS.RD2.104.545; RD2.105.209]

MARTIN, WILLIAM, a merchant in Dumfries in 1622. [NRS.E71.10.5]

MARTIN, WILLIAM, the younger, a merchant in Dumfries, a deed, 1715. [NRS.RD4.117.1093]

MASSIE, Lieutenant THOMAS, in Dumfries, testament, 1791, Comm. Dumfries. [NAS]

MASSON, JAMES, a cordiner in Bridgend of Dumfries, subscribed to the Test Act, 1683. [RPCS.VIII.641]

MASON, WILLIAM, a shoemaker, was admitted as a burgess of Dumfries in 1743. [DBR]

MAULE, MARIA, in Dumfries, 1781. [NRS.CS228.B7.35]

MAULE, Lieutenant THOMAS, in Dumfries, testament, 1791, Comm. Dumfries. [NRS]

MAXWELL, ALEXANDER, a workman, was admitted as a burgess of Dumfries in 1738. [DBR]

MAXWELL, ALEXANDER, a tailor, was admitted as a burgess of Dumfries in 1750. [DBR]

MAXWELL, ANNE, in Dumfries, relict of John Welsh, testament, 1773, Comm. Dumfries. [NRS]

MAXWELL, Major BRYCE, of the 8th Regiment of Foot, son of Provost Edward Maxwell and his wife Charlotte Blair, died 1809 in Martinique. [St Michael's MI, Dumfries]

MAXWELL, EDWARD, of the Hills, residing in Dumfries, suspected of Catholicism, 1601. [RPCS.VI.312]

MAXWELL, EDWARD, a merchant in Dumfries, deeds, 1715, [NRS.RD4.117.566/791]; testaments, 1743, 1753, 1756, and 1758, Comm. Dumfries. [NRS]

MAXWELL, EDWARD, a merchant, was admitted as a burgess of Dumfries in 1753. [DBR]

MAXWELL, EDWARD, late Provost of Dumfries, testament, 1791, Comm. Dumfries. [NRS]

MAXWELL, EDWARD, a merchant in Dumfries, sequestration, 1806. [NRS.DI.8.CCXX.149]

MAXWELL, ELIZABETH, spouse of Thomas Kirkpatrick a cordiner burgess of Dumfries, testament, 1656, Comm. Dumfries. [NRS]

MAXWELL, ELIZABETH, in Dumfries, relict of Reverend William Irvine, testament, 1781, Comm. Dumfries. [NRS]

MAXWELL, GEORGE, a burgess of Dumfries, testament, 1683, Comm. Dumfries. [NRS]

MAXWELL, FRANCIS, a smith, was admitted as a burgess of Dumfries in 1764. [DBR]

MAXWELL, GRISSEL, spouse of James Young a surgeon burgess of Dumfries, testament, 1628, Comm. Dumfries. [NRS]

MAXWELL, HARBERT, of Green Merse, a burgess of Dumfries, testament, 1629, Comm. Dumfries. [NRS]

MAXWELL, HOMER, Commissary of Dumfries, 1600. [RPCS.VI.636]

MAXWELL, HOMER, a merchant in Dumfries, testament, 1746, Comm. Dumfries. [NRS]

MAXWELL, HUGH, a writer in Dumfries, 1789. [NRS.CS228.B7.54.2]

MAXWELL, ISOBEL, relict of Richard Herries late Deacon of the Tailors of Dumfries, testament, 1678, Comm. Dumfries. [NRS]

MAXWELL, JAMES, a merchant in Dumfries, trading with La Rochelle, 1631. [NRS.AC7.2.386]; 1622; [NRS.E71.10.5]

MAXWELL, JAMES, clerk of the Fleshers of Dumfries, died 1678. [DAC]

MAXWELL, JAMES, a notary in Dumfries, testament, 1680, Comm. Dumfries. [NRS]

MAXWELL, JAMES, a wright in Dumfries, testament, 1724, 1727, Comm. Dumfries. [NRS]

MAXWELL, JAMES, a weaver, was admitted as a burgess of Dumfries in 1750. [DBR]

MAXWELL, JANET, relict of John Neilson a merchant in Dumfries, testament 1737, Comm. Dumfries. [NRS]

MAXWELL, Mr JOHN, residing in Dumfries, suspected of Catholicism, 1601. [RPCS.VI.312]

MAXWELL, JOHN, of Barncleugh, was appointed Provost of Dumfries in 1686 by King James VII. [RPCS.XIII.43]

MAXWELL, JOHN, a surgeon in Dumfries, testament [missing] 1697, Comm. Dumfries. [NRS]

MAXWELL, JOHN, of Barncleugh, a Roman Catholic in Dumfries, an apostate, with his daughter Mary, and his wife Margaret Young, 1704. [NRS.CH1.5.2]

MAXWELL, JOHN, of Middlenbie, in Dumfries, 1707. [EUL.LC. 3036]

MAXWELL, JOHN, a merchant, was admitted as a burgess of Dumfries in 1739. [DBR]; a merchant in Dumfries, heir to his father Edward Maxwell a merchant bailie of Dumfries in 1742, [NRS.S/H]; testaments, 1751, 1753, and 1759, Comm. Dumfries. [NRS]

MAXWELL, JOHN, a wright, was admitted as a burgess of Dumfries in 1742. [DBR]

MAXWELL, JOHN, a flesher, was admitted as a burgess of Dumfries in 1764. [DBR]

MAXWELL, JOHN, a merchant, was admitted as a burgess of Dumfries in 1773. [DBR]

MAXWELL, JOHN, a weaver, was admitted as a burgess of Dumfries in 1773. [DBR]

MAXWELL, JOHN, at the Bridgend of Dumfries, testament, 1796, Comm. Dumfries. [NRS]

MAXWELL, MAWSIE, servant to Hob McKie a burgess of Dumfries, 1599. [RPCS.VI.11]

MAXWELL, ROBERT, a merchant burgess of Dumfries, 1623. [NRS.GD6.1463]

MAXWELL, ROBERT, a merchant, was admitted as a burgess of Dumfries in 1739. [DBR]; a merchant in Dumfries, trading with Rotterdam, 1746. [NRS.E504.9.1]

MAXWELL, ROBERT, a coppersmith, was admitted as a burgess of Dumfries in 1752. [DBR]

MAXWELL, ROBERT, a workman, was admitted as a burgess of Dumfries in 1757. [DBR]

MAXWELL, ROBERT, of Cargen, a merchant in Dumfries, a bond, 1765. [NRS.RD2.197.242]

MAXWELL, ROBERT, and EDWARD, in Dumfries, letters, 1757-1759. [NRS.RH15.66.4]

MAXWELL, ROBERT, late Provost of Dumfries, testament, 1797, Comm. Dumfries. [NRS]

MAXWELL, THOMAS, a burgess of Dumfries, accused of liberating a prisoner from Dumfries Prison, 1600. [RPCS.VI.636]

MAXWELL, THOMAS, son of Thomas Maxwell a merchant burgess of Dumfries, was apprenticed to Adam Maxwell a merchant in Edinburgh on 9 April 1645. [Edinburgh Register of Apprentices]

MAXWELL, THOMAS, a merchant in Dumfries, husband of Agnes Irvine, and son John, a deed, 1714. [NRS.RD4.114.1017]

MAXWELL, WILLIAM, a barber, and his wife …..More, Roman Catholics in Dumfries, 1704. [NRS.CH1.5.2]

MAXWELL, WILLIAM, in Dumfries, a letter, 1732. [NRS.RH15.120.188]

MAXWELL, WILLIAM, a gentleman from Dumfries, a Jacobite of the French Royal Scots Cavalry, son of James Maxwell of Barncleugh, imprisoned as a rebel in 1746-1747. [SHS.3.16]

MAXWELL, WILLIAM, master of the Nanny and Jenny of Dumfries, trading with Virginia and Maryland in 1750. [NRS.E504.9.2]

MAXWELL and HUNTER, merchants in Dumfries, ledgers, 1732-1740. [NRS.CS96.1334.1/2]

MEAN, ALEXANDER, a writer in Dumfries, letters, 1742-1745. [NRS.GD78.22;0]; testaments, 1745, 1746, and 1750, Comm. Dumfries. [NRS]

MEIN, WILLIAM, a bookseller, was admitted as a burgess of Dumfries in 1739. [DBR]

MEIN, WILLIAM, a weaver, was admitted as a burgess of Dumfries in 1750. [DBR]

MENZIES, Dr JOHN, a physician in Dumfries, testament, 1725, Comm. Dumfries. [NRS]

MENZIES, THOMAS, an Excise officer in Dumfries, a deed, 1714. [NRS.RD2.103.2.228]

MERCER, CHARLES, a mathematician and master of the writing school in Dumfries, husband of Mary Grierson, parents of Agnes, Anna, Helen, James, and Mary, sasines, 1763-1772. [NRS.RS23.XIX.485, etc]; testament, 1784, Comm. Dumfries. [NRS]; born 1698, died 13 July 1772. [St Michael's MI]

MERCER, JAMES, son of Charles Mercer a mathematician in Dumfries, a mariner, a sasine, 1772. [NRS.RS23.XIX.15]

MERCER, MARY, daughter of Charles Mercer, mathematician in Dumfries, and spouse of James Morine MD in Jamaica, a sasine, 1772. [NRS.RS23.XXI. 15]

MILLER, ELIZABETH, in Dumfries, daughter of the late John Miller of Kirkgunzeon, testament, 1781, Comm. Dumfries. [NRS]

MILLER, JAMES, a shopkeeper, was admitted as a burgess of Dumfries in 1768. [DBR]

MILLER, RICHARD, an inn-keeper in Dumfries, was admitted as a burgess of Dumfries in 1767. [DBR]; a sasine, 1770. [NRS.RS23.XX.263]

MILLER, ROBERT, a tobacconist in Dumfries, 1786. [NRS.CE51.Letterbook]

MILLIGAN, BESSIE, in Dumfries, testament, 1661, Comm. Dumfries. [NRS]

MILLIGAN, ICHABOD, a shopkeeper, was admitted as a burgess of Dumfries in 1744. [DBR]; a merchant in Dumfries, testament, 1784, Comm. Dumfries. [NRS]

MILLIGAN, JAMES, a heritor of Dumfries, 1699. [NRS.CS36M.1/6]

MILLIGAN, JAMES, a surveyor in Dumfries, testament [missing] 1711, Comm. Dumfries. [NRS]

MILLIGAN, JAMES, an innkeeper, was admitted as a burgess of Dumfries in 1743. [DBR]

MILLIGAN, JAMES, a shopkeeper, was admitted as a burgess of Dumfries in 1762. [DBR]

MILLIGAN, JAMES, an innkeeper, was admitted as a burgess of Dumfries in 1799. [DBR]

MILLIGAN, JOHN, a merchant burgess of Dumfries, testaments, 1682 and 1685. Comm. Dumfries. [NRS]

MILLIGAN, JOHN, a merchant in Dumfries, testament, 1746, Comm. Dumfries. [NRS]

MILLIGAN, LILIAN, a servant to a merchant in Dumfries, guilty of infanticide, transported aboard the Rainbow and landed at Port Hampton, Virginia, 3 May 1775. [NRS.JC27.10.3]

MILLIGAN, ROBERT, a tobacconist in Dumfries, 1786. [NRS.CE51.Letterbook]

MILLIGAN, ROBERT, a merchant in Dumfries, 1788. [NRS.CS230.SEQNS.MC.1.3]

MILLIGAN, THOMAS, born 1785, a plumber in Dumfries, died 1857, husband of Allison Wight Anderson, parents of Robert Milligan who died in New York aged 37. [Dumfries MI]

MILLIGAN, WILLIAM, a weaver in Dumfries, sentenced to transportation to the colonies for rioting, shipped aboard the Matty and landed at Port Oxford, Maryland, 17 December 1771. [NRS.JC27.10.3; JC27.36.427]

MILLIGAN, WILLIAM, in the Kirkgate of Dumfries, testament, 1795, Comm. Dumfries. [NRS]

MILN, CHARLES, a tailor, was admitted as a burgess of Dumfries in 1740. [DBR]

MIRRIE, THOMAS, a merchant in Dumfries in 1622. [NRS.E71.10.2]

MIRRIE, THOMAS, a merchant in Dumfries, 1732. [NRS.E365.3]

MITCHELL, ALEXANDER, a weaver, was admitted as a burgess of Dumfries in 1742. [DBR]

MITCHELL, ARCHIBALD, a surgeon in Dumfries, 1727/1728. [NRS.AC9.979/1055]

MITCHELL, DAVID, a weaver, was admitted as a burgess of Dumfries in 1750. [DBR]

MITCHELL, JAMES, a merchant in Dumfries, a deed, 1714.
[NRS.RD2.103.2.573]

MITCHELL, JOHN, an innkeeper, was admitted as a burgess of Dumfries in
1799. [DBR]

MITCHELL, MARY, widow of George Anderson a wright in Dumfries,
testament, 1770, Comm. Dumfries. [NRS]

MITCHELL, WILLIAM, an innkeeper, was admitted as a burgess of Dumfries
in 1799. [DBR]

MITCHELL, WILLIAM, a merchant, was admitted as a burgess of Dumfries in
1799. [DBR]

MITCHELSON, ALEXANDER, of Carcrogo, born 1738, died 30 March 1789.
[St Michael's MI, Dumfries]

MITCHELSON, ARTHUR, born 1748, a dyer in Dumfries, died 16 January
1820, husband of Helen Grierson, parents of William Mitchelson born 1798, of
the Bengal Medical Staff, died 27 March 1866. [St Michael's MI, Dumfries]

MITCHELSON, CHARLES, a weaver in Dumfries, 1758. [NRS.CS271.45886]

MITCHELSON, JAMES, a merchant in Dumfries, and part-owner of the Ann
and Margaret 1727. [NRS.AC9.979/1038; AC8.353]; heir to his father John
Mitchelson a merchant in Dumfries, 1734. [NRS.S/H]

MITCHELSON, JAMES, a jeweller, was admitted as a burgess of Dumfries in
1739. [DBR]

MITCHELSON, JOHN, born 1658, died 31 August 1708. [St Michael's MI]

MITCHELSON, JOHN, a merchant in Dumfries, husband of Elizabeth Shortrig,
deeds, 1714, 1715, [NRS.RD2.103.2.694; RD2.104.1007]; testament, 1717,
1736, Comm. Dumfries. [NRS]

MITCHELSON, JOHN, a merchant in Dumfries, testament, 1745, Comm.
Dumfries. [NRS]

MITCHELSON, MARY, daughter of the deceased John Mitchelson a merchant
in Dumfries, testament, 1717, Comm. Dumfries. [NRS]

MITCHELSON, WILLIAM, a dyer, was admitted as a burgess of Dumfries in 1737. [DBR]

MOAT, JAMES, a baxter in Dumfries, testament [missing] 1714, Comm.Dumfries. [NRS]

MOAT, THOMAS, a barber and wigmaker in Dumfries, testament, 1741, Comm. Dumfries. [NRS]

MOFFAT, ALEXANDER, a merchant, was admitted as a burgess of Dumfries in 1745. [DBR]

MOFFAT, FRANCIS, a weaver, was admitted as a burgess of Dumfries in 1750. [DBR]

MOFFAT, GEORGE, a merchant in Dumfries, testament, 1687, Comm. Dumfries. [NRS]

MOFFAT, JAMES, a merchant in Dumfries in 1621. [NRS.E71.10.5]

MOFFAT, JOHN, son of the deceased George Moffat in Dumfries, testament, 1690, Comm. Dumfries. [NRS]

MOFFAT, JOHN, a baker, was admitted as a burgess of Dumfries in 1761. [DBR]

MONKHOUSE, WILLIAM, a hatter, was admitted as a burgess of Dumfries in 1773. [DBR]

MONTGOMERY, KATHERINE, arrived in Dumfries from Ireland in 1690. [NRS.CH2.537.15.1/27]

MONTGOMERY, ROBERT, a merchant in Dumfries, husband of Sarah Rome, inventory, 1713. [NRS.GD78.205]

MOORE, WILLIAM, a merchant in Dumfries, testament, 1800, Comm. Dumfries. [NRS]

MOORHEAD, JAMES, a merchant in Dumfries, testament, 1740, Comm. Dumfries. [NRS]

MOORHEAD, JAMES, a smith, was admitted as a burgess of Dumfries in 1770. [DBR]

MORISON, JOHN, a sailor in Dumfries, son of William Morison in Glenhead, testament, 13 January 1752, Comm. Dumfries. [NRS]

MORRINE, JAMES, a flesher, was admitted as a burgess of Dumfries in 1764. [DBR]

MORRINE, JOHN, a flesher in Dumfries, testament, 1735, Comm. Dumfries. [NRS]

MORRINE, MARGARET, in Dumfries, testament, 1682, Comm. Dumfries. [NRS]

MORRINE, WILLIAM, born 1781 in Dumfries, a storekeeper, died 10 August 1805 in Savanna, Georgia. [Georgia Courier, 4.9.1805; Savanna Death Register]

MORRISON, CHRISTIAN, relict of John Paul a merchant burgess of Dumfries, testament, 1628, Comm. Dumfries. [NRS]

MORRISON, ISABEL, relict of Gilbert McClene a merchant burgess of Dumfries, testament, 1642, Comm. Dumfries. [NRS]

MORRISON, JOHN, a merchant in Dumfries, testaments, 1745, 1746, and 1748, Comm. Dumfries. [NRS]

MORRISON, JOHN, a sailor in Dumfries, son of William Morrison in Glenhead, testament, 1752, Comm. Dumfries. [NRS]

MORRISON, JOHN, sometime a merchant in Antigua, thereafter in Dumfries, testament, 1770, Comm. Dumfries. [NRS]

MORRISON, THOMAS, a surgeon in Dumfries, testament, 1782, Comm. Dumfries. [NRS]

MORTON, ELIZABETH, spouse of Alexander Fairbairn a locksmith in Dumfries, testament, 1686, Comm. Dumfries. [NRS]

MORTON, ROBERT, a webster at the Bridgend of Dumfries, testament 1657, Comm. Dumfries. [NRS]

MUIR, P., a tobacconist in Dumfries, 1786. [NRS.CE51.Letterbook]

MUIR, ROBERT, born 1748, a merchant from Dumfries, settled in Virginia 1740, died 1786. [Christchurch MI, Virginia]

MUIR, ROBERT, an innkeeper, was admitted as a burgess of Dumfries in 1770. [DBR]

MUIR, ROBERT, a bricklayer, was admitted as a burgess of Dumfries in 1773. [DBR]

MUIRHEAD, DAVID, a merchant burgess of Dumfries, testament, 1674, Comm. Dumfries. [NRS]

MUIRHEAD, GEORGE, a surgeon apothecary in Dumfries, nephew of Robert Edgar minister at Maxton, a deed, 1714. [NAS.RD4.114.1059]

MUIRHEAD, JAMES, late bailie of Dumfries, testament,1685, Comm. Dumfries. [NRS]

MUIRHEAD, JAMES, senior, a merchant in Dumfries, 1733. [NRS.AC8.470]

MUIRHEAD, JAMES, junior, a merchant in Dumfries, 1733. [NRS.AC8.470]

MUIRHEAD, JOHN, a merchant in Dumfries, a decreet, 1723. [NRS.GD18.2578]

MUIRHEAD, MARGARET, relict of Andrew Sproat a mason in Dumfries, testament, 1764, Comm. Dumfries. [NRS]

MULLIGAN, JAMES, a surveyor in Dumfries, died August 1707. [NRS.GD3.2.87]

MUNCIE, GEORGE, a workman, was admitted as a burgess of Dumfries in 1753. [DBR]

MUNCIE, JAMES, a tailor burgess of Dumfries, testament, 1686, Comm. Dumfries. [NRS]

MUNCIE, JOHN, a flesher, was admitted as a burgess of Dumfries in 1754. [DBR]

MUNCIE, JOHN, a flesher, was admitted as a burgess of Dumfries in 1772. [DBR]

MUNCIE, JOHN, a flesher, was admitted as a burgess of Dumfries in 1793. [DBR]

MUNCIE, THOMAS, a carrier, was admitted as a burgess of Dumfries in 1743. [DBR]

MUNDELL, FRANCIS, a shoemaker, was admitted as a burgess of Dumfries in 1755. [DBR]

MUNDALL, JAMES, son of John Mundall Deacon of the Shoemakers in Dumfries, heir to his uncle Robert Mundall a writer in Dumfries, in 1748. [NRS.S/H]

MUNDELL, JOHN, residing in Dumfries, suspected of Catholicism, 1601. [RPCS.VI.312]

MUNDELL, JOHN, from Dumfries, a member of the Scots Charitable Society of Boston in 1694. [NEHGS/SCS]

MUNDELL, JOSEPH, was admitted as a burgess of Dumfries in 1744. [DBR]

MUNDELL, ROBERT, a writer in Dumfries, letters, 1730-1734. [NRS.GD47.465]; testaments, 1740 and 1748, Comm. Dumfries. [NRS]

MUNDELL, WILLIAM, merchant and late treasurer of Dumfries, testaments, 1716 and 1722, Comm. Dumfries. [NRS]

MURDO, JOHN, son of Robert Murdo a tailor burgess of Dumfries, was apprenticed to James Forsyth a merchant in Edinburgh on 16 October 1605. [Edinburgh Register of Apprentices]

MURDOCH, JOHN, a shoemaker, was admitted as a burgess of Dumfries in 1764. [DBR]

MURDOCH, MARION, in Dumfries, testament,1761, Comm. Dumfries. [NRS]

MURRAY, AGNES, in Dumfries, testament,1724, Comm. Dumfries. [NRS]

MURRAY, JOHN, a merchant in Dumfries, a deed, 1715. [NRS.RD4.116.741]

MURRAY, JOHN, a weaver, was admitted as a burgess of Dumfries in 1747. [DBR]

MURRAY, JOHN, a carter, was admitted as a burgess of Dumfries in 1749. [DBR]

MURRAY, JOHN, a weaver, was admitted as a burgess of Dumfries in 1771. [DBR]

MURRAY, ROBERT, a barber, was admitted as a burgess of Dumfries in 1762. [DBR]

MURRAY, WILLIAM, a merchant in Dumfries, a sasine, 1701.
[NRS.RH8.1037]

MURPHY, JOHN, a cooper, was admitted as a burgess of Dumfries in 1747.
[DBR]

MUTTER, THOMAS, born 1702, son of Reverend John Mutter, educated at
Edinburgh University, minister of St Michael's, Dumfries, from 1765 until his
death on 25 December 1793. Husband of [1] Isobel Balcanquhal, [2] Isobel
Costine, father of Jean, Elizabeth, Isobel, John, Isobel, and Eleanor. [F.2.266]

NAIRN, ROBERT, a skipper in Dumfries, master of the Thomas and James,
1741. [NRS.AC9.1471]

NAIRN, THOMAS, a saddler, was admitted as a burgess of Dumfries in 1745.
[DBR]

NAIRN, THOMAS, tidesman at the port of Dumfries, 1784, [NRS.E51.2/3];
testament 1795, Comm. Dumfries. [NRS]

NAIRN, THOMAS, a saddler, was admitted as a burgess of Dumfries in 1798.
[DBR]

NAPIER, ALEXANDER, a shoemaker, was admitted as a burgess of Dumfries
in 1760. [DBR]

NAPIER, JAMES, a shoemaker, was admitted as a burgess of Dumfries in
1750. [DBR]

NEILIE, SAMUEL, arrived in Dumfries from Ireland in 1690.
[NRS.CH2.537.15.1/30]

NEILL, JAMES, a merchant in Dumfries, a deed, 1714. [NRS.RD2.103.2.573]

NEILSON, GEORGE, a bailie of Dumfries, 1683. [RPCS.VIII.152]

NEILSON, JAMES, a messenger in Dumfries, 1743. [NRS.CS181.715]

NEILSON, JOHN, a tailor burgess of Dumfries, 1601. [RPCS.VI.263]

NEILSON, JOHN, a merchant in Dumfries, testament [missing] 1714, Comm.
Dumfries. [NRS]

NEILSON, JOHN, a writer in Dumfries, a deed, 1714. [NRS.RD2.103.2.560]

NEILSON, JOHN, a weaver, was admitted as a burgess of Dumfries in 1745. [DBR]

NEILSON, JOHN, a cooper, was admitted as a burgess of Dumfries in 1793. [DBR]

NEILSON, ROBERT, a tidewaiter at the port of Dumfries, testament, 1779, Comm. Dumfries. [NRS]

NEILSON, WALTER, a merchant in Dumfries, 1723, [NRS.AC9.820]; testaments, 1737, 1737, 1744, and 1747, Comm. Dumfries. [NRS]

NEILSON, WILLIAM, Dean of Guild in Dumfries, was accused of allowing a prisoner to escape from Dumfries Tolbooth in 1683. [RPCS.VIII.152]; a deed 1697. [NRS.RD2.80/1.603]

NEILSON, WILLIAM, the elder, a merchant in Dumfries, testament, 1722, Comm. Dumfries. [NRS]

NEWALL, ANDREW, a weaver, was admitted as a burgess of Dumfries in 1768. [DBR]

NEWALL, ANDREW, a Customs officer at Dumfries, 1784. [NRS.CE51.2/3]

NEWALL, HELEN, relict of Andrew Corsbie a merchant burgess of Dumfries, testament, 1675, Comm. Dumfries. [NRS]

NEWALL, HOMER, a weaver, was admitted as a burgess of Dumfries in 1760. [DBR]

NEWALL, HOMER, a tobacconist in Dumfries, 1786. [NRS.CE51.Letterbook]

NEWALL, JAMES, a bailie burgess of Dumfries, accused of liberating a prisoner from Dumfries Prison, 1600. [RPCS.VI.636]

NEWALL, JAMES, a smith burgess of Dumfries, testament, 1657, Comm. Dumfries. [NRS]

NEWALL, JAMES, a shopkeeper, was admitted as a burgess of Dumfries in 1767. [DBR]

NEWALL, JOHN, a notary burgess of Dumfries, an assignation, 1630. [NRS.GD5.113]

NEWALL, JOHN, a messenger in Dumfries, a deed, 1699. [NRS.RD2.83.562]; 1691. [RPCS.XIII.62]

NEWALL, JOHN, a shoemaker, was admitted as a burgess of Dumfries in 1738. [DBR]

NEWALL, MARTIN, a bailie of Dumfries, testaments [missing] 1700, 1710, Comm. Dumfries. [NRS]

NEWALL, ROBERT, a tailor, was admitted as a burgess of Dumfries in 1748. [DBR]

NEWALL, WILLIAM, a merchant in Dumfries in 1621 [NRS.E71.10.5]

NEWALL, WILLIAM, a shoemaker, was admitted as a burgess of Dumfries in 1750. [DBR]

NEWALL, WILLIAM, a merchant, was admitted as a burgess of Dumfries in 1750. [DBR]

NEWLANDS, JAMES, a bailie of Dumfries in 1683, accused of allowing a prisoner to escape from Dumfries Tolbooth. [RPCS.VIII.152]

NEWLANDS, JANET, spouse of Thomas Gourlay a burgess of Dumfries, testament, 1628, Comm. Dumfries. [NRS]

NICHOLSON, JAMES, a tobacconist in Dumfries, 1786. [NRS.CE51.Letterbook]

NICOLSON, JONATHAN, a tobacconist, was admitted as a burgess of Dumfries in 1754. [DBR]

NICOLSON, JOSEPH, a saddler, was admitted as a burgess of Dumfries in 1767. [DBR]; in Dumfries, testament, 1779, Comm. Dumfries. [NRS]

NICOLSON, JOSEPH, a smith, was admitted as a burgess of Dumfries in 1773. [DBR]

NICOLSON, THOMAS, a merchant in Dumfries, son and heir of the late Joseph Nicolson a saddler in Dumfries, testament, 1795, Comm. Dumfries. [NRS]

NISH, or MCNISH, SALLY, daughter of David Nish or McNish, merchant at the Bridgend of Dumfries, Versus Alexander Douglas, Lieutenant of the 46th Regiment, a process of divorce, 1798. [NRS.CC8.6.10.39]

NIXON, THOMAS, a horse-hirer, was admitted as a burgess of Dumfries in 1771. [DBR]

NORVAL, ROBERT, a baxter, was admitted as a burgess of Dumfries in 1766. [DBR]

NORVAL, WILLIAM, a baxter, was admitted as a burgess of Dumfries in 1742. [DBR]; in Dumfries, testament, 1766, Comm. Dumfries. [NRS]

OGILVIE, DAVD, a shoemaker, was admitted as a burgess of Dumfries in 1739. [DBR]

ORR, JOHN, a shoemaker, was admitted as a burgess of Dumfries in 1773. [DBR]

OUCHTERLONIE, JAMES, in Dumfries, bills of exchange, 1711-1716. [NRS.GD180.299]

OUGHTERSON, JOHN, of Milnthird, a resident of Dumfries, testaments, 1799, Comm. Dumfries. [NRS]

PAGAN, ANNA, spouse of Charles Herries a smith in Dumfries, testament 1739, Comm. Dumfries. [NRS]

PAGAN, DAVID, a shopkeeper, was admitted as a burgess of Dumfries in 1767. [DBR]

PAGAN, JAMES, a workman, was admitted as a burgess of Dumfries in 1740. [DBR]

PAGAN, JOHN, in the Kirkgate of Dumfries, testament, 1779, Comm. Dumfries. [NRS]

PAIN, JEAN, relict of Richard Howat late in Bridgend of Dumfries, testament, 1775, Comm. Dumfries. [NRS]

PALMER, JOHN, a merchant in Dumfries in 1622. [NRS.E71.10.5]

PALMER, JOHN, a saddler, was admitted as a burgess of Dumfries in 1759. [DBR]

PALMER, ROBERT, Collector in North Carolina, was admitted as a burgess of Dumfries in 1752. [DBR]

PALMER, WILLIAM, a saddler, was admitted as a burgess of Dumfries in 1742. [DBR]

PARK, ELIZABETH, spouse of John Wallis a flesher burgess of Dumfries, testament, 1638. Comm. Dumfries. [NRS]

PATERSON, EDWARD, a merchant in Dumfries, testament [missing] 1702, Comm. Dumfries. [NRS]

PATERSON, JAMES, a stocking weaver, was admitted as a burgess of Dumfries in 1770. [DBR]

PATERSON, JAMES, a glover, was admitted as a burgess of Dumfries in 1791. [DBR]

PATERSON, JAMES, born 1767 in Dumfries, master of the brig Moses Gill settled in New York 1802-1815, moved to Mississippi, died there 1 May 1829. [ANY.I.349]

PATERSON, JOHN, a merchant in Dumfries, 1693. [NRS.GD19.131]; a deed, 1702. [NRS.RD4.90.1100]

PATERSON, JOHN, a shopkeeper, was admitted as a burgess of Dumfries in 1757. [DBR]

PATERSON, JOHN, a saddler and late Deacon Convenor of the Trades of Dumfries, testaments, 1778 and 1779, Comm. Dumfries. [NRS]

PATERSON, MARGARET, spouse of William Moffat a merchant burgess of Dumfries, testament,1679, Comm. Dumfries. [NRS]

PATTERSN, ROBERT, a merchant in Dumfries in 1622. [NRS.E71.10.5]

PATTERSON, SUSANNA, arrived in Dumfries from Ireland in 1690. [NAS.CH2.537.15.1/30]

PATTERSON, THOMAS, arrived in Dumfries from Ireland in 1690. [NAS.CH2.537.15.1/30]

PATERSON, THOMAS, a saddler in Dumfries, testament, 1797, Comm. Dumfries. [NRS]

PATISON, CUTHBERT, a merchant in Dumfries in 1621. [NRS.E71.10.5]

PATON, FRANCIS, Customs Surveyor in Dumfries, testament, 1759, Comm. Dumfries. [NRS][NRS.E504.9.1]

PATON, JAMES, a shopkeeper, was admitted as a burgess of Dumfries in 1761. [DBR]

PATON, JOHN, a weaver, was admitted as a burgess of Dumfries in 1749. [DBR]

PATON, MARY, widow of William Stewart, Customs Controller of Dumfries, testament, 1788, Comm. Dumfries. [NRS]

PATON, ROBERT, graduated MA from Edinburgh University in 1691, minister of St Michael's, Dumfries, from 1696 to 1735, husband of Jean, daughter of James Muirhead a bailie of Dumfries, [2] Elizabeth Osburn, [3] Elizabeth, daughter of William Fingass a bailie of Dumfries, father of Robert, William, Francis later Customs surveyor in Dumfries, John a limner in Dumfries, Sarah, Mary, Marion, etc., Robert Paton died 22 October 1738 aged 78, [F.2.266]; testament, 18 February 1740, Comm. Dumfries. [NRS]

PATON, WILLIAM, a tailor, was admitted as a burgess of Dumfries in 1738. [DBR]

PATON, WILLIAM, a writer in Dumfries, testaments, 1800, 1802, Comm. Dumfries. [NRS]

PEACOCK, DAVID, a shopkeeper, was admitted as a burgess of Dumfries in 1763. [DBR]

PEIL, JOHN, a chaise-driver in Dumfries, testament, 1792, Comm. Dumfries. [NRS]

PERCIVAL, JAMES, a flesher, was admitted as a burgess of Dumfries in 1769. [DBR]

PEYSTER, Colonel ARENT SCHUYLER, was admitted as a burgess of Dumfries in 1794. [DBR]

PHILIPSON, JOHN, master of the Three Brothers of Dumfries, trading with Bordeaux, France, 1682. [NRS.E72.6.7]

PHILIPSON, MICHAEL, an innkeeper in Dumfries, testament, 1790, Comm. Dumfries. [NRS]

PICKERSGILL, SIMON, a writer in Dumfries, testament, 1722, Comm. Dumfries. [NRS]

POE, JAMES, master of the Adventure of Dumfries 1770s. [PA.26]

PORTEOUS, ROBERT, a shopkeeper, was admitted as a burgess of Dumfries in 1757. [DBR]

PORTER, MARY, relict of James Clark a barber in Dumfries, testament, 1751, Comm. Dumfries. [NRS]

POTTS, JOHN, from Dumfries, died 15 February 1798 at Ballard's River, Clarendon, Jamaica. [AJ.2635]

POTT, WILLIAM, a burgess of Dumfries, testament, 1641, Comm. Dumfries. [NRS]

POTT. WILLIAM, a smith, was admitted as a burgess of Dumfries in 1762. [DBR]

PRIMROSE, PETER, a shoemaker, was admitted as a burgess of Dumfries in 1750. [DBR]

PRINGALL, ROBERT, a Customs officer at Dumfries, 1613-1615. [NRS.E74.1.4; E74.2.4]

PRITCHARD, DAVID, master of the Margaret of Dumfries, 1689. [NRS.E72.6.13]

PURDIE, ISIOT, spouse to John Carlyle a workman in Dumfries, testament, 1676, Comm. Dumfries. [NRS]

PURSE, WALTER, in Dumfries, testament, 1680, Comm. Dumfries. [NRS]

QUEEN, JAMES, a hatter, was admitted as a burgess of Dumfries in 1786. [DBR]

QUEEN, JOHN, a hatter, was admitted as a burgess of Dumfries in 1737. [DBR]

QUEEN, JOHN, a hatter, was admitted as a burgess of Dumfries in 1786. [DBR]

QUHINCERSTANES, ROBERT, a burgess of Dumfries, was assaulted and mutilated in Dumfries 3 February 1601. [RPCS.VI.263]

RAE, ALEXANDER, a watchmaker, was admitted as a burgess of Dumfries in 1740. [DBR]

RAE, ARCHIBALD, a burgess of Dumfries, testament, 1661, Comm. Dumfries. [NRS]

RAE, FERGUS, a flesher, was admitted as a burgess of Dumfries in 1749. [DBR]

RAE, JOHN, a merchant in Dumfries in 1621. [NRS.E71.10.5]

RAE, JOHN, a flesher burgess of Dumfries, testament, 1627, Comm. Dumfries. [NRS]

RAE, JOHN, a merchant in Dumfries, 1723, [NRS.AC11.26]; a memorial, 1744. [NRS.RH18.3.117]

RAE, MARGARET, relict of William Beatty a smith in Dumfries, testament, 1734, Comm. Dumfries. [NRS]

RAE, MATHEW, a shoemaker, was admitted as a burgess of Dumfries in 1750. [DBR]

RAE, WILLIAM, a merchant formerly in Preston, then in Dumfries, 1711. [NRS.AC9.387]

RAINING, HERBERT, a burgess of Dumfries, husband of Malie Kirkpatrick, testament, 1600, Comm. Edinburgh. [NRS]

RAINING, JAMES, a merchant in Dumfries, testament, 1686, Comm. Dumfries. [NRS]

RAINING, JOHN, a shoemaker, was admitted as a burgess of Dumfries in 1746. [DBR]

RAMSAY, ..., son of Robert Ramsay, [1739-1810], and his wife Jean Malcolm, [1740-1820], died in New Providence aged 3. [Dumfries MI]

RAINING, JOHN, eldest son of the late John Raining a merchant burgess of Dumfries, testament, 1638, Comm. Dumfries. [NRS]

RAINING, THOMAS, burgh officer of Dumfries, testament, 1678, Comm. Dumfries. [NRS]

RALLING, CATHERINE, servant to James Maxwell a merchant burgess of Dumfries, testament, 1642, Comm. Dumfries. [NRS]

RAMMEIS, JOHN, a burgess of Dumfries, testament, 1600, Comm. Dumfries. [NRS]

RAMSAY, JAMES, Excise collector in Dumfries, 1771. [NRS.CS271.43782]; in Dumfries, 1786. [NRS.CE51.Letterbook]; testament, 1788, Comm. Dumfries. [NRS]

RAMSAY, JOHN, a writer in Dumfries, 1789. [NRS.CS228.B7.54.2]

RAMSAY, PETER, acting Supervisor of Excise in Dumfries, 1786. [NRS.CE51.Letterbook]

RAMSAY, WILLIAM, Commissary Clerk of Dumfries, 1648. [RGS.IX.2159]

RAWLING, THOMAS, a merchant in Dumfries, testament [missing] 1696, Com. Dumfries. [NRS]

REDPATH, WILLIAM, a merchant in Dumfries in 1621. [NRS.E71.10.5]

REID, DAVID, a merchant bailie of Dumfries, testaments, 1719, 1750, Comm. Dumfries. [NRS]

REID, FRANCIS, a tobacconist in Dumfries, 1786. [NRS.CE51.Letterbook]

REID, JAMES, a shopkeeper, was admitted as a burgess of Dumfries in 1757. [DBR]

REID, JOHN, born 1661, a bailie of Dumfries, died 20 May 1700. [St Michael's MI]; testaments [missing] 1700, 1709, 1710, Comm. Dumfries. [NRS]

REID, JOHN, a merchant from Dumfries, settled in Virginia, 1740, died in Norfolk, Va., 1791. [SM.53.568]

REID, MATHEW, and Margaret Reid, children of the late John Reid a bailie of Dumfries, testament [missing] 1713, Comm. Dumfries. [NRS]

REID, THOMAS, a breeches maker, was admitted as a burgess of Dumfries in 1773. [DBR]

REID, WILLIAM, a smith, was admitted as a burgess of Dumfries in 1742. [DBR]; Deacon of the Hammermen of Dumfries, testament, 1778, Comm. Dumfries. [NRS]

RENNICK, JOHN, a tobacconist in Dumfries, 1727. [NRS.AC9.1015]

REOCH, PATRICK, an Excise officer in Dumfries, testament, 1738, Comm. Dumfries. [NRS]

RICHARDS, EDWARD, a riding officer at the port of Dumfries, testament, 1759, Comm. Dumfries. [NRS]

RICHARDSON, AGNES, spouse of John Gilchrist late Baillie of Dumfries, testament, 1690, Comm. Dumfries. [NRS]

RICHARDSON, JOHN, a merchant burgess of Dumfries, 1622, [NAS.E71.10.5]; testament, 1658, Comm. Dumfries. [NRS]

RICHARDSON, JOHN, the younger, a merchant in Dumfries, testament, 1681, Comm. Dumfries. [NRS]

RICHARDSON, JOHN, a merchant in Dumfries, a deed, 1702. [NRS.RD4.90.1182]

RICHARDSON, JOHN, a tailor, was admitted as a burgess of Dumfries in 1768. [DBR]

RICHARDSON, JOHN, in Dumfries, testament, 1773, Comm. Dumfries. [NRS]

RICHARDSON, JOSEPH, master of the Foam of Dumfries, 1786. [NRS.CE51.Letterbook]

RICHARDSON, ROBERT, a baxter, was admitted as a burgess of Dumfries in 1762. [DBR]

RICHARDSON, SARA, in Dumfries, letters, 1719-1737. [NRS.RH15.120.175]

RICHARDSON, THOMAS, treasurer of Dumfries, 1683. [RPCS.VIII.152]

RICHARDSON, THOMAS, a merchant in Dumfries, testament, 1687, Comm. Dumfries. [NRS]

RICHARDSON, WILLIAM, a merchant burgess of Dumfries, testament, 1628, Comm. Dumfries. [NRS]

RICHARDSON, WILLIAM, in Dumfries, 1800. [NRS.CS234.SEQN.R.1.24]

RIDDELL, WAUCHOPE, in Dumfries, daughter of Robert Riddell of Glenriddell, testament, 1792, Comm. Dumfries. [NRS]

RIDDELL, Mrs WAUCHOPE, in Dumfries, daughter of Walter Riddell, testament, 1799, Comm. Dumfries. [NRS]

RIDDICK, JOHN, a tailor, was admitted as a burgess of Dumfries in 1749. [DBR]

RIDDICK, ROBERT, of Corbiton, in Dumfries, testament, 1799, Comm. Dumfries. [NRS]

RIGG, EDWARD, son of Robert Rigg a wright burgess of Dumfries, was apprenticed to William Brand a wright in Edinburgh on 26 December 1655. [Edinburgh Register of Apprentices]

RIGG, GEORGE, a merchant in Dumfries in 1622. [NRS.E71.10.5]; testament, 1637, Comm. Dumfries. [NRS]

RIGG, ROBERT, a wright at the Bridgend of Dumfries, married Elspet Maxwell, a Roman Catholic on 17 November 1633, contrary to law, consequently he was imprisoned in Edinburgh Tolbooth. [RPCS.V.262]

ROAN, JOHN, a shoemaker, was admitted as a burgess of Dumfries in 1778. [DBR]; in Dumfries, inhibition, 1797. [NRS.D1.127/1.212/15]

ROBERTSON, DAVID, a currier, was admitted as a burgess of Dumfries in 1773. [DBR]; in Dumfries, testament, 1790, Comm. Dumfries. [NRS]

ROBERTSON, GEORGE, a merchant in Dumfries, 1791. [NRS.CS96.824]

ROBERTSON, JAMES, a baxter, was admitted as a burgess of Dumfries in 1738. [DBR]

ROBERTSON, WILLIAM, a tobacconist in Dumfries, 1786. [NRS.CE51.Letterbook]

ROBISON, ANDREW, a merchant in Dumfries, testaments [missing] 1703, 1706, Comm.Dumfries. [NRS]

ROBISON, ANDREW, a barber, was admitted as a burgess of Dumfries in 1737. [DBR]

ROBSON, ANDREW, a merchant in Dumfries, a deed, 1691.
[NRS.RD4.68.226]; testament, 1692, Comm. Dumfries. [NRS]

ROBSON, JAMES, a merchant in Dumfries, husband to Janet Lockhart, Parents of James, Thomas, and Margaret, 1693. [EUL.LC2908]

ROBSON, JAMES, a merchant in Dumfries, a deed, 1691. [NRS.RD2.73.586]

ROBSON, JAMES, a tobacconist in Dumfries, 1786. [NRS.CE51.Letterbook]

ROBSON, JOHN, sr., a merchant in Dumfries, testament [missing] 1709, Comm. Dumfries. [NRS]

ROBSON, WILLIAM, a hatter, was admitted as a burgess of Dumfries in 1755. [DBR]

RODGER, WILLIAM, master of the Margaret of Dumfries, 1690. [NRS.E72.6.18]

RODDICK, JOHN, a shopkeeper, was admitted as a burgess of Dumfries in 1767. [DBR]

ROGERSON, THOMAS, a merchant in Dumfries, testament, 1730, Comm. Dumfries. [NRS]

ROME, GEORGE, a merchant burgess of Dumfries, husband of Bessie Maxwell, tacks, 1651. [NRS.RH9.17.437]

ROME, GEORGE, a writer in Dumfries, 1707. [EUL.MS3036]

ROME, JOHN, a merchant in Dumfries in 1621, trading with Flanders in 1622. [NRS.E71.10.5]

ROME, JOHN, a bailie of Dumfries in 1683, 1686, 1687. [RPCS.VIII.152; XIII.43/172/205]

ROME, JOHN, a merchant burgess of Dumfries, baron of Dalswinton-Rome, and his sons John and Robert, 1703. [NRS.86.814]

RONALD, JOHN, a weaver, was admitted as a burgess of Dumfries in 1742. [DBR]

RORISON, JAMES, a merchant, was admitted as a burgess of Dumfries in 1739. [DBR]

ROSS, GEORGE, a merchant, was admitted as a burgess of Dumfries in 1773. [DBR]

ROSS, JOHN, a surgeon apothecary, sometime in Dumfries, testament, 1724, Comm. Dumfries. [NRS]

ROSS, JOHN, born 1725, a surgeon, died 25 May 1750. [St Michael's MI]

ROSS, WALTER, a shipmaster in Dumfries, testaments, 1742, 1744, Comm. Dumfries. [NRS]

ROWAN, JAMES, a flesher, was admitted as a burgess of Dumfries in 1738.. [DBR]

ROWAN, JAMES, sailor in Dumfries, son of Reverend James Rowan, testament, 1750, Comm. Dumfries. [NRS]

ROWLANDSON, JAMES, a farrier, was admitted as a burgess of Dumfries in 1737. [DBR]

RULE, JAMES, a tailor, was admitted as a burgess of Dumfries in 1749. [DBR]

RULE, JOHN, an apothecary in Dumfries, testament [missing] 1702, Comm. Dumfries. [NRS]

RULE, JOHN, a merchant in Dumfries, a petition, 1764. [NRS.RH18.3.92]

RULE, ROBERT, a notary burgess of Dumfries, testament, 1657, Comm. Dumfries. [NRS]

SANDERS, JAMES, a weaver, was admitted as a burgess of Dumfries in 1768. [DBR]

SCHAW, JOHN, a merchant in Dumfries in 1621. [NRS.E71.10.5]

SCOTLAND, HENRY, a gardener in Wellgreen, Dumfries, testament, 1781, Comm. Dumfries. [NRS]

SCOTT, ADAM, a merchant in Dumfries in 1622. [NRS.E71.10.5]

SCOTT, ALEXANDER, minister of Greyfriars, Dumfries, from 1770 to 1806. [F.2.269]

SCOTT, FRANCIS, a merchant in Dumfries, later in Virginia, versus Elizabeth Wright, widow of Thomas Kirkpatrick, a merchant in Dumfries, 8 June 1748. [NRS.CS16.1.80]

SCOTT, JANET, spouse of John Wilson a weaver in Dumfries, testament, 1657, Comm. Dumfries. [NRS]

SCOTT, JOHN, late Deacon of the Shoemakers of Dumfries, testament, 1676, Comm. Dumfries. [NRS]

SCOTT, JOHN, arrived in Dumfries from Ireland during 1690. [NRS.CH2.537.1/127]

SCOTT, JOHN, born 1697, minister of Greyfriars, Dumfries, from 1732 until his death 17 April 1770. Husband of Christian Wardrop, parents of John, and William born 8 August 1738, died 15 September 1764 in Charleston, South Carolina. [F.2.269]

SCOTT, JOHN, a watchmaker, was admitted as a burgess of Dumfries in 1773. [DBR]

SCOTT, JOHN, a carter in Dumfries, testament, 1794, Comm. Dumfries. [NRS]

SCOTT, ROBERT, master of the Mariann of Dumfries, 1689. [NRS.E72.6.20/21]

SCOTT, WALTER, a merchant in Dumfries in 1621. [NRS.E71.10.5]

SCOTT, WALTER, a shoemaker, was admitted as a burgess of Dumfries in 1799. [DBR]

SCOTT, WILLIAM, a vintner in Dumfries, 1717. [NRS.GD52.1474]; testaments, 1749, 1750, Comm. Dumfries. [NRS]

SCOTT, WILLIAM, a merchant from Dumfries, settled in Charleston, South Carolina, in 1750s, probate South Carolina, 1765. [SCGaz]

SELKIRK, WILLIAM, a flesher, was admitted as a burgess of Dumfries in 1764. [DBR]

SHARP, GEORGE, a merchant burgess of Dumfries, testament, 1640, Comm. Dumfries. [NRS]

SHARP, JOHN, late bailie of Dumfries, testament, 1675, Comm. Dumfries. [NRS]

SHARP, JOHN, heir to his father John Sharp a merchant bailie of Dumfries, 1656. [NRS,Retours, Dumfries.229]

SHARP, JOHN, of Hoddam, late Sheriff and Commissary Clerk of Dumfries, testaments, 1723, 1744, 1759, Comm. Dumfries. [NRS]

SHARP, JOHN, merchant in Dumfries, a deed, 1691. [NRS.RD4.69.37]

SHARP, JOHN, clerk of Dumfries, 1691. [RPCS.XVI.62]

SHARP, THOMAS, a merchant burgess of Dumfries, husband of Margaret Beck, testament, 1627, Comm. Dumfries. [NRS]

SHARP, THOMAS, of Houstoun, was admitted as a burgess of Dumfries, 1741. [NRS.GD30.1925]

SHORT, FRANCIS, writer in Dumfries, 1787. [NRS.CS221.B7.35]

SHORTRIG, ELIZABETH, relict of John Mitchelson a merchant in Dumfries, a deed, 1715. [NRS.RD2.105.352]

SHORTRIG, JAMES, a merchant in Dumfries, husband of Margaret McNaught, 1698. [NRS.RH8.260.1]

SHORTRIG, JOHN, late Convenor of the Trades in Dumfries, 1687. [RPCS.XIII.156]

SHORTRIG, JOHN, at the Bridgend of Dumfries, testament, 1736, Comm. Dumfries. [NRS]

SHORTRIG, NICOLA, spouse to John Shortrig, the elder, late Deacon of the Glovers, testament, 1684, Comm. Dumfries. [NRS]

SHORTRIG, ROBERT, at the Bridgend of Dumfries, testament, 1689, Comm. Dumfries. [NRS]

SHORTRIG, THOMAS, a baxter, was admitted as a burgess of Dumfries in 1765. [DBR]

SHORTRIG, WILLIAM, a burgess of Dumfries, 1600. [RPCS.VI.636]

SIMPSON, ROBERT, a nailer, was admitted as a burgess of Dumfries in 1759. [DBR]

SIMPSON, THOMAS, an innkeeper. was admitted as a burgess of Dumfries in 1761. [DBR]

SIMPSON, THOMAS, a vintner in Dumfries, testament, 1762, Comm. Dumfries. [NRS]

SLOAN, DAVID, a breeches maker, was admitted as a burgess of Dumfries in 1799. [DBR]

SLOAN, THOMAS, a baxter, was admitted as a burgess of Dumfries in 1737. [DBR]

SMART, JAMES, a carpenter in Dumfries, testament, 1690, Comm. Dumfries. [NRS]

SMITH, ELIZABETH, in Dumfries, testament, 1792, Comm. Dumfries. [NRS]

SMITH, FRANCIS, a staymaker, was admitted as a burgess of Dumfries in 1765. [DBR]

SMITH, JAMES, a merchant in Dumfries, 1707. [EUL.LC3036]

SMITH, JAMES, a writer in Dumfries, was admitted as a burgess of Dumfries in 1737. [DBR]

SMITH, JAMES, a chapman in Dumfries, testament, 1764, Comm. Dumfries. [NRS]

SMITH, JAMES, a hostler, was admitted as a burgess of Dumfries in 1786. [DBR]

SMITH, JOHN, in Dumfries, testament, 1736, Comm. Dumfries. [NRS]

SMITH, JOHN, a weaver, was admitted as a burgess of Dumfries in 1742. [DBR]

SMITH, JOHN, a weaver, was admitted as a burgess of Dumfries in 1750. [DBR]

SMITH, JOHN, a flesher, was admitted as a burgess of Dumfries in 1763. [DBR]

SMITH, JOHN, a tailor, was admitted as a burgess of Dumfries in 1766. [DBR]

SMITH, JOHN, hostler at the King's Arms Inn of Dumfries, testament, 1777, Comm. Dumfries. [NRS]

SMITH, JOHN, an innkeeper in Dumfries, testament, 1781, Comm. Dumfries. [NRS]

SMITH, JOHN, of the Jerusalem Arms, was admitted as a burgess of Dumfries in 1794. [DBR]

SMITH, LEONARD, a flesher, was admitted as a burgess of Dumfries in 1763. [DBR]

SMITH, ROBERT, a merchant burgess of Dumfries, a disposition, 1624. [NRS.GD10.217]

SMITH, ROBERT, a merchant burgess of Dumfries, testament, 1658, Comm. Dumfries. [NRS]

SMITH, SAMUEL, master of the Jenny of Dumfries trading with Danzig in 1754. [NRS.E504.9.2]

SMITH, SAMUEL, a shopkeeper, was admitted as a burgess of Dumfries in 1769. [DBR]

SMITH, THOMAS, a spirits dealer, was admitted as a burgess of Dumfries in 1798. [DBR]

SMITH, WILLIAM, a flesher, was admitted as a burgess of Dumfries in 1737. [DBR]

SMITH, WILLIAM, a merchant in Dumfries, testament, 1766, Comm. Dumfries. [NRS]

SMITH, WILLIAM, born 1717 in Dumfries, died 1768 in New York. [Matthew's American Armory and Blue Book, London, 1903]

SOMERVILLE, JOHN, a writer in Dumfries, deeds, 1697, 1715, [NRS.RD2.81/1.438; RD4.116.1135; RD4.116.973]; testaments [missing] 1699, 1705, Comm. Dumfries.[NRS]

SPENS, JOHN, a merchant burgess of Dumfries in 1621, [NRS.E71.10.5]; testament, 1638, Comm. Dumfries. [NRS]

SPENS, MARGARET, spouse of Harbert Morrison a merchant burgess of Dumfries, testament, 1624, Comm. Dumfries. [NRS]

SPENS, MARGARET, spouse of George Neilson a merchant burgess of Dumfries, testaments, 1642, 1643, Comm. Dumfries. [NRS]

SPROAT, MARGARET, spouse to John Goldie a merchant burgess of Dumfries, testament, 1625, Comm. Dumfries. [NRS]

STAIG, DAVID, a Collector in Dumfries, 1786. [NRS.CE51.Letterbook]

STEVENSON, or KENNEDY, ALEXANDER, a fencing and dancing master in Dumfries, married in April 1714 in Dumfries to Mary Rogerson, Process of Divorce, 12 March 1726. [NRS.CC8.6.222]

STEILL, GAVIN, a merchant in Dumfries in 1622. [NRS.E71.10.5]

STEILL, SIMON, a merchant in Dumfries in 1622. [NRS.E71.10.5]

STEVENSON, PETER, a smith, was admitted as a burgess of Dumfries in 1770. [DBR]

STEWART, ARCHIBALD, a merchant in Dumfries, testament, 1738, Comm. Dumfries. [NRS]

STEWART, JAMES, a merchant in Dumfries, testaments,1731 and 1735, Comm. Dumfries. [NRS]

STEWART, THOMAS, born 1777 in Dumfries, an architect in Augusta, Georgia, died in Camp Hope, Milledgeville, Georgia, in August 1826. [Georgia Republican. 30 September 1826]

STEWART, WILLIAM, Customs controller in Dumfries, letter, 1744. [NRS.GD110.617]; testaments, 1762, 1777, Comm. Dumfries. [NRS]

STONE, RICHARD, a merchant in Dumfries, 1727. [NRS.AC9.1015]

STORIE, GEORGE, a merchant in Dumfries, a deed, 1691. [NRS.RD3.75.496]

STORY, JOHN, a writer, was admitted as a burgess of Dumfries in 1751. [DBR]

STOTHART, THOMAS, of Arkland, a writer, was admitted as a burgess of Dumfries in 1766. [DBR]; in Dumfries, testament,1792, Comm. Dumfries. [NRS]

STOTT, JOHN, a merchant burgess of Dumfries, testament, 1686, Comm. Dumfries. [NRS]

STRANGE, ELIZABETH, a spinning mistress in Dumfries, testament, 1748, Comm. Dumfries. [NRS]

STURGEON, JAMES, a sailor in Dumfries, testament, 1735, Comm. Dumfries. [NRS]

STURGEON, JAMES, a mariner in Dumfries, 1741, [NRS.AC9.1471]; shipmaster in Dumfries, residing in Righead, testament, 1751, Commissariat of Dumfries. [NRS]

STURGEON, JAMES, an innkeeper in Dumfries, testament, 1793, Comm. Dumfries. [NRS]

STURGEON, MARY, widow of James Sturgeon an innkeeper in Dumfries, 1794. [NRS.CS228.B9.19]

STURGEON, WILLIAM, a shopkeeper in Dumfries, testament, 1760, Comm. Dumfries. [NRS]

SUTHERLAND, THOMAS, master of the Friendship of Dumfries, testaments, 1735, 1738, Comm. Dumfries. [NRS]

SUTHERLAND, WILLIAM, a landwaiter in Dumfries, testament, 1729, Comm. Dumfries. [NRS]

SWAN, JAMES, in Dumfries, testament, 1763, Comm. Dumfries. [NRS]

SWAN, JOHN, Deacon of the Wrights of Dumfries, testament, 1731, Comm. Dumfries. [NRS]

SWAN, JOHN, a writer, was admitted as a burgess of Dumfries in 1750. [DBR]

SWAN, WILLIAM, a wigmaker in Dumfries, testaments, 1733, Comm. Dumfries. [NRS]

TAIT, ARCHIBALD, a workman, was admitted as a burgess of Dumfries in 1761. [DBR]

TAIT, EBENEZER, an innkeeper, was admitted as a burgess of Dumfries in 1770. [DBR]

TAIT, THOMAS, a carpenter in Dumfries, testament [missing] 1708, Comm. Dumfries. [NRS]

TAIT, Messrs and Company, tobacconists in Dumfries, 1786. [NRS.CE51.Letterbook]

TAYLOR, BESSIE, spouse of James Tait a merchant burgess of Dumfries, testament, 1629, Comm. Dumfries. [NRS]

TAYLOR, JAMES, a staymaker, was admitted as a burgess of Dumfries in 1747. [DBR]

TAYLOR, DOUGAL, master of the Esther of Dumfries, trading with Rotterdam and Cork, 1754. [NRS.E504.9.2]

TAYLOR, JAMES, late hospital mate of the 96th Regiment of Foot, son of the late William Taylor in Dumfries, testament, 1799, Comm. Dumfries. [NRS]

TAYLOR, JOHN, Deacon of the Wrights of Dumfries, testament, 1649, Comm. Dumfries. [NRS]

TAYLOR, WILLIAM, a watchmaker, was admitted as a burgess of Dumfries in 1769. [DBR]

THOMAS, WILLIAM, son of William Thomas a merchant in Dumfries, a thief, transported from Dumfries aboard the Kirkconnell of Dumfries bound for Virginia, 1715. [DGA.GF4.19A.10]

THOMSON, ABRAHAM, a chain and cart-wright, was admitted as a burgess of Dumfries in 1770. [DBR]

THOMSON, ADAM, a merchant in Dumfries, in 1621. [NRS.E71.10.5]

THOMSON, ARCHIBALD, a merchant in Dumfries, in 1621. [NRS.E71.10.5]

THOMSON, DAVID, a wright at the Bridgend of Dumfries, testament, 1689, Comm. Dumfries. [NRS]

THOMSON, JAMES, a burgess of Dumfries, testament, 1638, Comm Dumfries. [NRS]

THOMSON, JAMES, a smith, was admitted as a burgess of Dumfries in 1764. [DBR]

THOMSON, Captain JAMES, in Dumfries, testaments, 1798, 1799, Comm. Dumfries. [NRS]

THOMSON, JANET, spouse of William Grier a merchant burgess of Dumfries, testament, 1659, Comm. Dumfries. [NRS]

THOMSON, JANET, with Joan Thomson, and Marion Thomson, Romans Catholics in Rigside, Dumfries, 1704. [NRS.CH1.5.2]

THOMSON, JOHN, schoolmaster of Dumfries, testament, 1624, Comm. Dumfries. [NRS]

THOMSON, JOHN, schoolmaster of Dumfries, husband of Agnes Douglas, 1661. [NRS.RD3.1.501]

THOMSON, JOHN, a baker, was admitted as a burgess of Dumfries in 1771. [DBR]

THOMSON, JOHN, a merchant from Dumfries, settled in Halifax, North Carolina, by 1777. [TNA.AO12.102.125]

THOMSON, JOHN, a fish curer in Dumfries, 1786. [NRS.CE51.Letterbook]

THOMSON, RICHARD, a grocer, was admitted as a burgess of Dumfries in 1799. [DBR]

THOMSON, WALTER, a slater in Dumfries, 1727. [NRS.AC9.1015]

THOMSON, WILLIAM, a merchant in Dumfries, testament, 1728, Comm. Dumfries. [NRS]

THOMSON, WILLIAM, a plasterer, was admitted as a burgess of Dumfries in 1771. [DBR]

THORNEBRAND, MATTHEW, a merchant burgess of Dumfries, testament, 1679, Comm. Dumfries. [NRS]

THRASHIE, ROBERT, a tailor, was admitted as a burgess of Dumfries in 1764. [DBR]

TROTTER, ELIZABETH, arrived in Dumfries from Ireland in 1690. [NRS.CH2.537.15.1/30, 61]

TURNER, JAMES, an innkeeper, was admitted as a burgess of Dumfries in 1798. [DBR]

TURNER, WILLIAM, a tobacconist in Dumfries, testament, 1758, Comm. Dumfries. [NRS]

TWADDELL, ANDREW, a mason, was admitted as a burgess of Dumfries in 1759. [DBR]; Deacon of the Squaremen in Dumfries, 1770. [NRS.CS271.48481]; born 1735, died 9 October 1787. [St Michael's MI]

TWADDELL, THOMAS, born 1707, Deacon of the Squaremen of Dumfries, died 8 July 1762. [St Michael's MI]; testament, 1767, Comm. Dumfries. [NRS]

TWADDELL, THOMAS, a Customs officer at Dumfries, 1784. [NRS.CE51.2/3]; testament, 1794, Comm. Dumfries. [NRS]

TWEEDIE, JOHN, a merchant in Dumfries, deeds, 1702. [NRS.RD2.86.2.60; RD4.91.412]

VAIR, JAMES, a merchant in Dumfries, testament, 1732, Comm. Dumfries. [NRS]

VEITCH, JAMES, a shoemaker at the Bridgend of Dumfries, and his wife Mary Gass, a sasine 1772. [NRS.RS23.XXI.38/343]

VEITCH, THOMAS, a barber and wigmaker in Dumfries, testament, 1745, Comm. Dumfries. [NRS]

VEITCH, WILLIAM, minister in Dumfries, deeds, 1702. [NRS.RD2.86.1.21; RD4.90.632]; testament, 1724, Comm. Dumfries. [NRS]

VEITCH, THOMAS, a dyer at the Bridgend of Dumfries, husband of Marion Brown, a sasine, 1768. [NRS.RS23.XX,224]

VETCH, WILLIAM, born 27 April 1640, son of Reverend John Veitch in Roberton, graduated MA from Glasgow University in 1659, minister of St Michael's, Dumfries, from 1694 until 1715, died 8 May 1722, husband of Marion Fairley, parents of Captain William Veitch who died off Jamaica in 1699 on the Darien Expedition, Samuel, born 1668, Governor of Nova Scotia, died 30 April 1732, Ebenezer, Elizabeth, Sarah, Agnes, Janet, etc, [F.2.265]; letters, 1715. [NRS.GD220.5.578]; testament, 5 November 1724, Comm. Dumfries. [NRS]; deeds, 1715. [NRS.RD2.104.414/958]

VEITCH, WILLIAM, son of James Veitch, a merchant in Dumfries, a deed, 1715. [NRS.RD4.116.243]

WADDELL, PETER, son of William Waddell, a mason, [1712-1781], and his wife Jean Buttar, died in Jamaica aged 29. [Dumfries MI]

WADDELL, WILLIAM, a mason, was admitted as a burgess of Dumfries in 1737. [DBR]

WALKER, ADAM, residing in Dumfries, suspected of Catholicism, 1601. [RPCS.VI.312]

WALKER, ARCHIBALD, son of Robert Walker, [1735-1805], and his wife Herries Gray, died 5 February 1805 in Virginia. [Dumfries MI]

WALKER, ADAM, burgess of Dumfries, accused of liberating a prisoner from Dumfries Prison, 1600. [RPCS.VI.636]

WALKER, JAMES, a merchant in Dumfries, 1746. [NRS.AC11.168]

WALKER, JOHN, a tailor, was admitted as a burgess of Dumfries in 1740. [DBR]

WALKER, JOHN, a butcher, was admitted as a burgess of Dumfries in 1764. [DBR]

WALKER, THOMAS, a skinner, was admitted as a burgess of Dumfries in 1771. [DBR]

WALKER, WILLIAM, born 1760, late in St Thomas in the East, Jamaica, died 27 October 1820. [Dumfries MI]

WALKER, ..., a merchant in Dumfries, 1786. [NRS.CE51.Letterbook]

WALL, ROBERT, a tanner, was admitted as a burgess of Dumfries in 1769. [DBR]

WALL, ROBERT, [1781-1846], father of Philip Wall who died in Jamaica aged thirty-three., also of William Henry Wall, who died in Port Morant, Jamaica aged twenty-five. [Dumfries MI]

WALLACE, DAVID, a dyer in Dumfries, subscribed to the Test, 1683. [RPCS.VIII.641]; a witness in 1687. [RPCS.XIII.156]

WALLACE, GRIZEL, spouse of William Sympson a glazier in Dumfries, testament, 1683, Comm. Dumfries. [NRS]

WALLACE, JAMES, an innkeeper, was admitted as a burgess of Dumfries in 1798. [DBR]

WALLACE, JANET, a widow in Dumfries, aged 45, a witness in 1687. [RPCS.XIII.171]

WALLACE, JOHN, merchant in Dumfries, 1744, [NRS.AC9.1515]; sometime a merchant in Dumfries, testament, 1770, Comm. Dumfries. [NRS]

WALLACE, JOHN, a shoemaker, was admitted as a burgess of Dumfries in 1762. [DBR]

WALLACE, JOHN, an innkeeper, was admitted as a burgess of Dumfries in 1767. [DBR]

WALLACE, RACHEL, relict of John Irving late Baillie of Dumfries, testaments, 1718 and 1719, Comm. Dumfries. [NRS]

WALLET, MARY, wife of James Aitken convenor of the Trades of Dumfries, heir to her father John Wallet in Knockgee, in 1744. [NRS.S/H]

WALLS, JOHN, an Excise officer in Dumfries, 1786. [NRS.CE51.Letterbook]

WALTERET, ALEXANDER, a tailor, was admitted as a burgess of Dumfries in 1766. [DBR]

WALTNET, WILLIAM, a tailor, was admitted as a burgess of Dumfries in 1749. [DBR]

WARD, HUGH, a joiner, was admitted as a burgess of Dumfries in 1743. [DBR]

WATSON, ANDREW, a joiner, was admitted as a burgess of Dumfries in 1763. [DBR]; Deacon of the Squaremen of Dumfries, testament, 1794, Comm. Dumfries. [NRS]

WATSON, JANET, in Dumfries, testament, 1658, Comm. Dumfries. [NRS]

WATSON, ROBERT, a tailor, was admitted as a burgess of Dumfries in 1749. [DBR]

WATSON, WILLIAM, a shopkeeper, was admitted as a burgess of Dumfries in 1763. [DBR]

WAUGH, ROBERT, at the Bridgend of Dumfries, husband of Agnes Colvin, sasines, 1770s. [NRS.RS23.XX.346; XXI.40]

WEIR, JOHN, absconded from Dumfries to Ireland in 1692. [NRS.CH2.537.15.2/145-146]

WEEMS, JAMES, a watchmaker, was admitted as a burgess of Dumfries in 1786. [DBR]

WEEMS, JEAN, a milliner in Dumfries, 1782. [NRS.CS228.W. 3.85.2]

WEEMS, JOHN, a skinner, was admitted as a burgess of Dumfries in 1759. [DBR]

WEEMS, WILLIAM, a wright, was admitted as a burgess of Dumfries in 1742. [DBR]

WEIR, JAMES, a merchant in Dumfries, testament, 1795, Comm. Dumfries. [NRS]

WELES, JOHN, a flesher burgess of Dumfries, testament, 1659, Comm. Dumfries. [NRS]

WELLIS, GEORGE, a chapman in Dumfries, testament, 1682, Comm. Dumfries. [NRS]

WELLS, GEORGE, a merchant in Dumfries, a deed, 1714. [NRS.RD4.114.369-374]; testament, [missing] 1711, Comm. Dumfries. [NRS]

WELSH, ALEXANDER, a shoemaker, was admitted as a burgess of Dumfries in 1765. [DBR]

WELSH, EDWARD, a merchant in Dumfries, testament, 1745, Comm. Dumfries. [NRS]

WELSH, JOHN, of Milton, a writer in Dumfries, husband of Susanna McWilliam, sasines, 1767-1778. [NRS.RS23.XX.124, etc]

WELSH, THOMAS, a merchant, was admitted as a burgess of Dumfries in 1771. [DBR]

WELSH, WILLIAM, a surgeon apothecary in Dumfries, testaments, 1787 and 1790, Comm. Dumfries. [NRS]

WELSH, WILLIAM, a flesher, was admitted as a burgess of Dumfries in 1797. [DBR]

WEMYSS, JAMES, late watchmaker in Dumfries, now in Langholm, versus Eliza Mitchell or Mitchelson, seamstress in Dumfries, his spouse, married 1787. Process of Divorce, 1790. [NRS.CS221.21]

WEMYSS, JOHN, a tidewaiter, was admitted as a burgess of Dumfries in 1740. [DBR]

WHARRIE, EDWARD, in Dumfries, testament, 1763, Comm. Dumfries. [NRS]

WHITE, JOHN, a cooper, was admitted as a burgess of Dumfries in 1740. [DBR]

WHITE, JOHN, a mason in Dumfries, a testament, 1752, Comm. Dumfries. [NRS]

WIGHT, ROBERT, born 1684, son of William Wight, a tenant in Glengelt, Channelkirk, and his wife Janet Somerville, graduated MA from Edinburgh University in 1703, minister of St Michael's, Dumfries, from 1732 until 1730, he died 4 December 1764. He married Jean Robson in 1726, parents of Jean, William, Belle, Janet, Margaret, Mary, Helen, Alison, and Robert. [F.2.266]

WIGHTMAN, WILLIAM, a linen draper in Dumfries, testament, 1771, Comm. Dumfries. [NRS]

WILKIE, ANDREW, a barber, was admitted as a burgess of Dumfries in 1738. [DBR]

WILKIE, HUGH, a carter, was admitted as a burgess of Dumfries in 1761. [DBR]

WILKIE, THOMAS, a cooper, was admitted as a burgess of Dumfries in 1742. [DBR]

WILKINE, MARGARET, relict of John Lewars a merchant burgess of Dumfries, testament, 1679, Comm. Dumfries. [NRS]

WILLANE, ROBERT, a cutler, was admitted as a burgess of Dumfries in 1783. [DBR]

WILLIAMS, RODERICK, a merchant burgess of Dumfries, testament, 1674, Comm. Dumfries.[NRS]

WILLIAMSON, JOHN, a merchant in Dumfries trading with Flanders in 1622. [NRS.E71.10.5]

WILLIAMSON, JOHN, in Dumfries, a bond, 1634. [NRS.GD6.1905]

WILLIAMSON, JOHN, a merchant burgess of Dumfries, testament, 1683, Comm. Dumfries. [NRS]

WILLIAMSON, JOHN, a ropemaker in Dumfries, testament, 1800, Comm. Dumfries. [NRS]

WILLIAMSON, JOHN, a merchant in Dumfries, husband of Janet Martin, a sasine, 1764. [NRS.RS23.XIX.276]

WILLIAMSON, WILLIAM, a merchant in Dumfries in 1622. [NRS.E71.10.5]

WILSON, ALEXANDER, an Excise officer in Dumfries, testaments, 1739, Comm. Dumfries. [NRS]

WILSON, ANDREW, a merchant in Dumfries in 1621-1622. [NRS.E71.10.5]

WILSON, ANDREW, a tailor in Dumfries, sentenced to transportation to the colonies for rioting, shipped aboard the Matty and landed at Port Oxford, Maryland, 17 December 1771. [NRS.JC27.10.3; JC27.36.427]

WILSON, ANDREW, a baker in Dumfries, testaments, 1785, 1790, Comm. Dumfries. [NRS]

WILSON, DAVID, a flesher, was admitted as a burgess of Dumfries in 1738. [DBR]

WILSON, EBENEZER, a bookseller in Dumfries, testaments, 1790, 1791, Comm. Dumfries. [NRS]

WILSON, EPHRAIM, a merchant in Dumfries, testaments, 1732, 1751, Comm. Dumfries. [NRS]

WILSON, JAMES, a merchant burgess of Dumfries, testament, 1630, Comm. Dumfries. [NRS]

WILSON, JAMES, a tailor in Dumfries, testament, 1659, Comm. Dumfries. [NRS]

WILSON, JAMES, a tanner, was admitted as a burgess of Dumfries in 1762. [DBR]

WILSON, JAMES, innkeeper at the Bridgend of Dumfries, testament, 1777, Comm. Dumfries. [NRS]

WILSON, JANET, relict of Robert Bailie a merchant in Dumfries, sasines, 1705-1727. [NRS.RS23.7.108/163; 10/319]

WILSON, JANET, in Dumfries, relict of Duncan Robison a musician, a disposition, 1768. [NRS.GD314.121]

WILSON, JOHN, a merchant in Dumfries, in 1622. [NRS.E71.10.5]

WILSON, JOHN, an Exciseman in Dumfries, dead by 1773. [NRS.CS229.C3.44]; testament, 1753, Comm, Dumfries. [NRS]

WILSON, JOHN, a weaver, was admitted as a burgess of Dumfries in 1762. [DBR]

WILSON, JOHN, a shoemaker, was admitted as a burgess of Dumfries in 1767. [DBR]

WILSON, JOHN, of Bogrie, a merchant in Dumfries, 1786, [NRS.CE51.Letterbook]; testament, 1790, Comm. Dumfries. [NRS]

WILSON, MARGARET, spouse to John Wilson a merchant burgess of Dumfries, testament, 1678, Comm. Dumfries. [NRS]

WILSON, MATTHEW, a tobacconist in Dumfries, 1786. [NRS.CE51.Letterbook]

WILSON, NICOLA, spouse to John Dickson a cordiner in Dumfries, testament, 1685, Comm. Dumfries. [NRS]

WILSON, ROBERT, a chapman, was admitted as a burgess of Dumfries in 1742. [DBR]

WILSON, ROBERT, a tanner, was admitted as a burgess of Dumfries in 1761. [DBR]

WILSON, ROBERT, an innkeeper, was admitted as a burgess of Dumfries in 1768. [DBR]

WILSON, ROBERT, a gardener, was admitted as a burgess of Dumfries in 1773. [DBR]

WILSON, SAMUEL, a tailor, was admitted as a burgess of Dumfries in 1763. [DBR]

WILSON, THOMAS, a shoemaker, was admitted as a burgess of Dumfries in 1773. [DBR]

WILSON, THOMAS, a carter in Dumfries, testament, 1778, Comm. Dumfries. [NRS]

WILSON, WILLIAM, Deacon of the Tailors of Dumfries, and his spouse Jean Wilson, testament, 1682, Comm. Dumfries. [NRS]

WILSON, WILLIAM, a merchant in Dumfries, testament [missing] 1714, Comm. Dumfries. [NRS]

WILSON, WILLIAM, a skinner, was admitted as a burgess of Dumfries in 1759. [DBR]

WILSON, WILLIAM, a carter, was admitted as a burgess of Dumfries in 1760. [DBR]

WILSON, WILLIAM, a staymaker was admitted as a burgess of Dumfries in 1765. [DBR]; in Dumfries, testament, 1800, Comm. Dumfries. [NRS]

WILSON, WILLIAM, a gardener, was admitted as a burgess of Dumfries in 1786. [DBR]

WISHART, ANN, daughter of the late James Wishart a cooper in Dumfries, versus her husband William MacLachlan a journeyman slater in Edinburgh, married 1762. Process of Separation, 1766. [NRS.CC8.6.429]

WOOD, JAMES, a shopkeeper, was admitted as a burgess of Dumfries in 1798. [DBR]

WOOD, JONATHAN, a slater, was admitted as a burgess of Dumfries in 1773. [DBR]

WOOD, WILLIAM, a gardener, was admitted as a burgess of Dumfries in 1766. [DBR]

WOODMASS, JOHN, a skinner and gover at the Bridgend of Dumfries, a sasine, 1767. [NRS.RS23.XX.107]

WRANGHAM, ALEXANDER, a tidesman in Dumfries, 1741. [NRS.AC9.1515]

WRIGHT, AGNES, relict of William Douglas the burgh officer of Dumfries, testament, 1691, Comm. Dumfries. [NRS]

WRIGHT, ELIZABETH, widow of Thomas Kirkpatrick, a merchant in Dumfries, versus Francis Scott, a merchant in Dumfries, later in Virginia, 8 June 1748. [NRS.CS16.1.80]

WRIGHT, JOHN, a shoemaker, was admitted as a burgess of Dumfries in 1786. [DBR]

WRIGHT, JOHN, a tobacconist in Dumfries, 1786. [NRS.CE51.Letterbook]

WRIGHT, ROBERT, a carrier burgess of Dumfries, spouse of Margaret Anderson, testament, 1681, Comm. Dumfries.[NRS]

WRIGHT, ROBERT, a merchant, was admitted as a burgess of Dumfries in 1747. [DBR]

WRIGHT, ROBERT, a shoemaker, was admitted as a burgess of Dumfries in 1764. [DBR]

WRIGHT, ROBERT, a merchant in Dumfries, sasines, 1773. [NRS.RS23.XXI. 183/184/361]; testaments, 1783, 1787, Comm. Dumfries. [NRS]

WRIGHT, SAMUEL, master of the Robert of Dumfries, 1690. [NRS.E72.6.18]

WRIGHT, THOMAS, a merchant burgess of Dumfries, husband of Marion Beck, testament, 1638, Comm. Dumfries. [NRS]

WRIGHT, THOMAS, a merchant in Dumfries, testaments, 1704, 1713. Comm. Dumfries. [NRS]

WYLIE, ALEXANDER, a druggist in Dumfries, a sasine, 1778. [NRS.RS23.XXII.54]

WYLLIE, JAMES, a merchant in Dumfries, in 1622. [NRS.E71.10.5]

WYLLIE, JAMES, a watchmaker in Dumfries, husband of Janet Bishop, a sasine, ca1768. [NRS.RS23.XX.107]

WYLLIE, WILLIAM, a mason, was admitted as a burgess of Dumfries in 1738. [DBR]

YOUNG, ALEXANDER, born 1773, Speaker of the House of Assembly in New Providence, died 6 September 1813 in Nassau. [Dumfries MI]

YOUNG, GEORGE, a writer in Dumfries, testaments, 1753, 1759, Comm. Dumfries. [NRS]

YOUNG, ISABEL, relict of John Craik a merchant in Dumfries, testament, 1690, Comm. Dumfries. [NRS]

YOUNG, JOHN, Sheriff-Clerk of Dumfries, testament, 1628, Comm. Dumfries. [NRS]

YOUNG, JOHN, a slater burgess of Dumfries, testament, 1658, Comm. Dumfries. [NRS]

YOUNG, JOHN, Customs Collector at Dumfries. 1743. [NRS.E504.9.1]; testaments, 1759, 1775, Comm. Dumfries. [NRS]

YOUNG, PATRICK, a surgeon in Dumfries, in 1621. [RPCS.XII.586]

YOUNG, ROBERT, a surgeon burgess of Dumfries, a bond, 1649. [NRS.GD10.757]

YOUNGER, JOHN, a writer in Dumfries, and his spouse Elizabeth Copland, testament, 1747, Comm. Dumfries. [NRS]

CPSIA information can be obtained
at www.ICGtesting.com
Printed in the USA
FFOW01n1206050816
26455FF

9 780806 357782